The Poetry of
Georges Bataille

The Poetry of Georges Bataille

GEORGES BATAILLE

Translated and with an introduction by
STUART KENDALL

Original poems published in French by Éditions Gallimard (EG)

From *Œuvres complètes III* © Éditions Gallimard, 1971
  L'Être indifférencié n'est rien (pp. 367–76) ; « Poèmes disparates » (pp. 543–44)
From *Œuvres complètes IV* © Éditions Gallimard, 1971
  « Douleur et quatre poèmes » (pp. 11–13) ; « Je mets mon vit . . . » (p. 14) ; « O crâne . . . » (p. 15) ; « Onze poèmes retires de L'Archangélique » (pp. 16–19) ; « Poèmes éliminés » (pp. 20–26) ; « Le loup soupire . . . » (p. 27) ; « Poèmes érotiques » (pp. 28–32) ; « Coryphea » (p. 33) ; « Cinq poèmes de 1957 » (pp. 34–36) ; *La Tombe de Louis XXX* (pp. 153–54)
From *Œuvres complètes V* © Éditions Gallimard, 1973
  Poèmes tirés de *L'Expérience intérieure* (pp. 71–72, 121, 185–89) ; Poèmes tirés de *Le Coupable* (pp. 237, 314, 356–57)
From *Œuvres complètes VI* © Éditions Gallimard, 1973
  Poèmes tirés de *Sur Nietzsche* (pp. 80, 98–103)
From *Romans et récits*
  Être Oreste (pp. 578–94) © Éditions Gallimard, 1971 et 2004
From *L'Archangélique et autres poèmes*
  L'Archangélique (pp. 21–64) © Éditions Gallimard, 1967 ; « Dans le halo de *la* mort » (p. 144) © Éditions Gallimard, 1971 et 1973 ; « Acéphale » (p. 145) © Éditions Gallimard, 1971 et 1973

Published by State University of New York Press, Albany

© 2018 State University of New York

For information, contact State University of New York Press, Albany, NY
www.sunypress.edu

Library of Congress Cataloging-in-Publication Data

Names: Bataille, Georges, 1897–1962 author. | Kendall, Stuart translator author of introduction.
Title: The poetry of Georges Bataille / Georges Bataille ; translated and with an introduction by Stuart Kendall.
Description: Albany : State University of New York Press, 2018. | Includes bibliographical references and index.
Identifiers: LCCN 2018000358 | ISBN 9781438472317 (hardcover : alk. paper) | ISBN 9781438472324 (pbk. : alk. paper)
Classification: LCC PQ2603.A695 A2 2018 | DDC 841/.912—dc23
LC record available at https://lccn.loc.gov/2018000358

10   9   8   7   6   5   4   3   2   1

Contents

Translator's Introduction

The Hatred of Poetry

The poetic genius is not a verbal gift . . . it is the divination of ruins.

—Georges Bataille, *Inner Experience*

The reputation of Georges Bataille (1897–1962) rests most firmly on his extraordinary works of fiction, including *Story of the Eye*, *Blue of Noon*, and *Madame Edwarda*; his essays on general economy, *The Accursed Share* and *Eroticism*; and his all-but-unclassifiable volumes of philosophical autobiography, *Inner Experience*, *Guilty*, and *On Nietzsche*. To say that Bataille's poetry is less well known than these other works is to understate the matter.[1] This may be due in part to its relative scarcity. Though poetry figures in four of his major works, all of Bataille's poetry can be collected in one relatively slim volume.[2] Bataille's poetry never stood apart within his literary output: only 113 copies of his major poetic work, *Archangelic* (1944), were printed during his lifetime and those were distributed only to "friends" of the journal *Messages*, which published the book. Nevertheless poetry and the problem of poetic language played a crucial role in the development of Bataille's thought and writing. The publisher's advertising band wrapped around the first edition of Bataille's first book, *Inner Experience* (1943), proclaimed that book to be "Beyond Poetry" even though the book itself included several poems, most notably a concluding section consisting entirely of poems, written, as Bataille says, "with necessity—in accordance with my life."[3] Paradoxically, Bataille's turn to poetry coincided not only with the beginning of his career as a writer of books but also with a stance or outlook that is situated in some way beyond poetry.

Like much else in Bataille's thought and life, his poetry and his thought about poetry evidence the challenge signaled by the title of another of Bataille's books that includes poetry, *The Hatred of Poetry* (1947), a volume better known in English by the title Bataille gave it for its second edition, *The Impossible* (1962). Bataille explained both of these titles in the preface to that second edition: "It seemed to me that true poetry was reached only by hatred. Poetry had no powerful meaning except in the violence of revolt. But poetry attains this violence only by evoking the impossible."[4] In notes for that preface, he wrote: "*The Impossible* is still, is above all entirely complete violence and unlivable tragedy. It is that which exceeds the conventions of literary poetry."[5] Along similar lines, in *Method of Meditation*, a text written alongside the poetry of *The Impossible*, Bataille describes poetry and "poetic effusion" as a "sovereign behavior" alongside other ecstatic behaviors, intoxication, eroticism, laughter, and sacrifice, among others.[6] Poetry, in other words, and in Bataille's view, is a privileged mode of writing and of experience, a sovereign mode, a means of violence and revolt, but it is also rare, both within Bataille's oeuvre and otherwise. And if the word *poetry* as he uses it refers to a mode of writing that "exceeds the conventions of literary poetry," not all poetry meets this standard, or, more strongly put, is in fact poetry in this strict sense. Poetry, for Bataille and in short, is not merely beautiful language or finely wrought phrases. But if poetic language is neither everyday speech nor simply beautiful language, what exactly is it? And if it is as significant as Bataille suggests it is, why did it suffer such neglect in his life as a writer? When and why did he begin writing poetry and when and why did he stop?

Bataille turned to poetry quite late in his career and then still only for a relatively brief period of time. The first poems by Bataille that can be reliably dated appear as part of *Inner Experience*, a book he began writing in the fall of 1941, when he was already forty-four years old. In his youth and while still caught up in a fervent, if short-lived, Christian faith, Bataille wrote some poems in free verse on religious topics, one on the wartime destruction of the cathedral in Reims, the city where he spent most of his youth, and another on an imagined religious pilgrimage to Jerusalem.[7] Nevertheless, and not without significance, Bataille seems to have lost his faith in poetry alongside his faith in God during the early 1920s. Thereafter, despite his ongoing literary ambitions, poetry disappeared from his work for over twenty years. And yet, across those same twenty years, Bataille wrote a few of the most extraordinary literary texts of his century—*Story of the Eye* (1927), *Blue of Noon* (1935), and *Madame Edwarda* (1941)—as well as restlessly pushing the formal boundaries and philosophical resources of the critical essay, particularly in the fields of aesthetics and politics, in pieces published in the journals *Documents*, *La Critique Sociale*, and *Acéphale*.[8] Bataille's literary muse was, in other words, and somewhat obviously, otherwise engaged during those years. Nevertheless the absence of poetry during this period is notable not least because Bataille did eventually begin writing poems. Following the fall of 1941, and then more consistently over the next three years, Bataille wrote the majority of his poetry as well as perhaps his most searching reflections on poetry and poetic language. Why did this happen? Why only then, at that time?

Before turning to the specific circumstances of Bataille's own turn toward poetry, we can make some more broadly contextual observations regarding his friends and influences and the literary milieu in which he began writing poetry. In France between the wars, among the members of the aesthetic avant-garde, promiscuous formal experimentation was more common that it may be today. Bataille's closest friends and clearest intellectual interlocutors all wrote in a wide, indeed almost kaleidoscopically shifting variety of forms and genres: prose and poetry, novels and autobiography, criticism, reviews, philosophical or theoretical speculation, cultural critique and analysis. While some figures, like Paul Éluard, were undoubtedly known for one form of expression, in his case poetry, others, like Antonin Artaud or Henri Michaux, made significant contributions to culture in multiple distinct forms and indeed media, across the literary and visual arts. In each of these cases, restricting our appreciation of their works to one form or genre would profoundly limit our understanding of that work both as a whole and in part. Closer to Bataille, Michel Leiris, one of Bataille's close friends from the mid-1920s until the end of his life, wrote significant bodies of both poetry and prose, including his many volumes of anthropology and autobiography, most notably *Phantom Africa* (1934) and the four volume series *The Rules of the Game* (1948–76). Though renowned for his prose, Leiris continued to write and publish poetry throughout his life. Reflecting on the relationship between Bataille's writing practices and his inner circle of friends, we should also remember that at the time of her death, Bataille's lover, Colette Peignot, more commonly known by her middle name, Laure, left behind a small but powerful collection of poetry and prose writings, which Bataille and Michel Leiris printed privately in two small editions for limited circulation thereafter.[9] These publications, in 1939 and 1942, coincide, generally speaking, with Bataille's own turn toward poetry and are reflected, and in fact quoted, in his work.

Writing in a multitude of forms was of course not unique to the members of Bataille's generation and circle. The foremost influence on Bataille's thought and work was another writer who wrote in many genres and forms, Friedrich Nietzsche. As Bataille put it in *On Nietzsche*: "With few exceptions, my company on earth is that of Nietzsche. . . . My life in Nietzsche's company is a community; my book is this community."[10] To our current point, and despite recent attempts to confine his works to the philosophy section of libraries, Nietzsche too wrote in a variety forms. He wrote essays and aphorisms, intended for both professional and popular readerships, but also music and poetry, as well as what we might call philosophical poetry, for want of a better term for that work which stands altogether apart, *Thus Spoke Zarathustra* (1883–85). Georges Bataille began *Inner Experience* by situating it alongside Nietzsche's *The Gay Science* (1882) as a book wherein profundity and passion go hand in hand.[11] Nietzsche's *Gay Science* is of course also a book that begins with a "Prelude in Rhymes" and ends with an appendix of poems, the "Songs of Prince Vogelfrei." Nietzsche also included poems in several of his other works, as well as publishing his poems separately.[12] Bataille found many things in Nietzsche; one of those things was a stylistic precedent for including poetry in a volume of philosophical prose.

But again Nietzsche was not the only influence on Bataille whose writing combined multiple forms and registers. The major works of the great Carmelite mystic, St. John of the Cross, *The Ascent of Mount Carmel*, *The Dark Night of the Soul*, *The Spiritual Canticle*, and *The Living Flame of Love*, are structured as theological poems followed by detailed commentaries on those poems. St. John was an essential reference for Bataille, particularly in *Inner Experience*, where, speaking of methods of meditation, he admits: "I have followed his [St. John's meditational] method of hardening right to the end."[13] Far more even than Nietzsche, and far more than would be appropriate for us to demonstrate here, the works of St. John of the Cross influenced the language, form, and content of Bataille's poetry. The sensually visceral but spiritual landscape of St. John of the Cross—the dark night, the desperate spiritual isolation and ascent, the torturous burning and urgent longing of a lover for a beloved, the darkness and the light—are essential to Bataille's poetic language, purpose, and effect, though of course with a different final goal and ultimate meaning.

For St. John of the Cross and for Nietzsche, as for Bataille, the multiplication of forms and registers, in prose and poetry, served distinct necessities, evidenced distinct intentions and audiences as well as distinct orientations toward and ideas about the nature and purpose of writing. "Why write?" in cases such as these needs a supplemental precision: "Poetry? Prose? An essay? An aphorism?" In each case the answer is different. This difference becomes most apparent when the forms are mixed, pushed up against one another, or arranged or assembled in juxtaposition, alongside one another, in stark contrast.

Beyond these contemporaries and influences, Bataille consistently references the work of only a select few other poets, particularly in his books from the war years, when he was himself writing the majority of his poetry: William Blake, Emily Brontë, Edgar Allan Poe, Charles Baudelaire, le Comte de Lautréamont, Arthur Rimbaud, the French dramatist Jean Racine, and, often disparagingly, the surrealist poets, including André Breton. Later on, two of his contemporaries, Jacques Prévert and René Char, would be added to the list of poets and poetry that compelled Bataille's interest.[14] If we expand the list to include a few other names Bataille links in a positive way with the mechanisms of poetic language, Marcel Proust, Franz Kafka, Fyodor Dostoevsky, we have something like a kind of pantheon of poetry and literature for Bataille.[15] This list is significant for the specific names it includes as well as for its brevity.

Bataille's poets in particular are all accursed, *maudite*, poets associated with moral transgression and the notion of evil. In 1957, Bataille gathered some of his writings on Brontë, Baudelaire, Blake, Proust, and Kafka in his book of literary essays under the title, *Literature and Evil*.[16] His thoughts on the others more often appeared as stray remarks: "Poe and Baudelaire on the level of the impossible: I love them and burn with the same fire."[17] "Humility before Lautréamont or Rimbaud: a new form of unhappy consciousness, it has its pedants like the old kind."[18] "Lautréamont's *Poésies*, are they not literature 'pleading guilty'?"[19] "Lautréamont as bible of [*innocence?*] in reality this bible is once again ancient tragedy, poetry made by everyone."[20] But, whether in extended essays or stray remarks, the purpose and thrust of the association remained consistent: "Emily Brontë, of all women, seems to have been the object of a privileged curse. . . . Keeping her moral purity intact, she had a profound experience of the abyss of Evil."[21] "Blake managed, in phrases of a peremptory simplicity, to reduce humanity to poetry and poetry to Evil."[22]

These notions and associations were not original. Blake himself famously associated evil with energy and life: "the active[,] springing from Energy"; energy, for Blake, is "eternal delight."[23] Blake said of Milton: "The reason Milton wrote in fetters when he wrote of Angels & God and at liberty when of Devils & Hell, is because he was a true Poet and of the Devils party without knowing it."[24] Baudelaire's *Flowers of Evil* begin with a poem, "To the Reader," which counts among its admissions, the fact that the Devil pulls the poet's strings: "Each day we descend a step toward Hell, / Without horror, through the stinking darkness." Rimbaud's major work, *A Season in Hell*, sets out, at the end of its introduction, with an ambivalent cry: "But, dear Satan, I beg of you, a less irritated gaze! And while awaiting those few delayed infamies, for you who love in a writer the absence of descriptive or instructive abilities, I will tear out these few hideous pages from my notebook of the damned." One of the sections of *A Season in Hell* is entitled *The Impossible*.

Bataille's affinity for these accursed poets is almost overdetermined. The author of *Guilty* claimed: "Literature is not innocent. It is guilty and should admit itself so."[25] Such claims brought him in line with the accursed poets but also with a sensibility about art and literature that was common enough following the fin de siècle aesthetic movements of symbolism and decadence. Indeed, Bataille was part of a generation whose members brought avant-garde tendencies together in aesthetic, social, and political forms. Standing apart from society, rejecting norms of individual and social behavior, and seeking new political structures for communal life went hand in hand with a search for new aesthetic models for expression and experience. *Literature and Evil* begins with just such an admission: "I belong to a turbulent generation. . . . In the years after the Great War, there was a feeling which was about to overflow. Literature was stifling within its limitations and seemed pregnant with revolution."[26] The other members of that generation shared a sense of its genealogy and of the place of the accursed poets within that genealogy. Antonin Artaud—to name only one particularly turbulent member of that turbulent generation—often wrote of the impact of a nearly identical pantheon of figures on his own work: Baudelaire, Poe, Nerval, Rimbaud, Lautréamont, but also Kierkegaard, Nietzsche, Coleridge, and Hölderlin, among others.[27] Bataille too considered Nietzsche the "philosopher of evil."[28] From our distance it's almost too easy to perceive these figures as merely among the greatest innovators and most fecund writers of their times. But it's important to remember that they form a distinct countertradition, a tradition formed by writing through modes and mores in more or less direct opposition to the dominant literary and cultural traditions of their day. Nevertheless, by aligning himself with the legacy of the accursed poets, Bataille found himself in good company among the members of his own generation. One mark of Bataille's methods and purpose can be found in the extent to which he integrated the aesthetic, social, and political inheritance of these writers. He also explicitly eschewed originality and continued along the path these writers blazed. However anachronistically it may sound to our disenchanted ears, he confessed, in the accursed vein: "I believe that Evil—an acute form of Evil—which it expresses, has a sovereign value for us."[29] Or again, in *On Nietzsche*: "I make nothing less than *evil* the object of an extreme moral search."[30]

Most of Bataille's remarks about poetry and poets appear in his writings from the war years or later. Prior to the war, Bataille did not reference poetry regularly in his writing. He wrote primarily about visual forms in *Documents* and primarily about social thought in *La Critique Sociale*. Even when the reviews he wrote for *La Critique Sociale* did consider works of literature, they did so with a clear eye on the social implications of the work in question.[31] In the late 1930s, as Bataille's concerns moved more resolutely beyond visual culture and beyond the political, into the realm of religion and the sacred, he wrote respectfully of poetry "since Rimbaud" (Baudelaire and Gérard de Nerval are also mentioned in the notes) but nevertheless relegated "verbal invention" to the level of vanity and failure, mere "art." Bataille's search had pushed him well beyond the search for the beautiful and the true, whether in visual, verbal, or philosophical form, toward the region of a "privileged instant" that he identified with the experience of the sacred. In his essay, "The Sacred," written in November of 1938, as Laure lay dying, Bataille put forward the following assertion: "Whoever creates, whoever paints or writes, can no longer concede any limitations on painting or writing; *alone*, he suddenly has at his disposal all possible human convulsions, and he cannot flee from this heritage of divine power— which belongs to him. Nor can he try to know if this heritage will *consume* and *destroy* the one it *consecrates*. But he refuses now to surrender 'what possesses him' to the standards of salesmen, to which art has conformed."[32] Needless to say, the validation of the market held no meaning for Bataille during that period of his life, a period we may summarize under the heading of headlessness, Acéphale, in which experience alone was key. And yet, in that moment, and in the quotation above, we can also perceive a recognition on Bataille's part that modern art, including poetry, at least since Rimbaud, inherited a quest for an experience, however failed, of "fundamental importance for all life."[33]

Perhaps the first apotheosis of this search recorded in Bataille's published work appears in his 1939 program piece, "The Practice of Joy before Death." The piece begins with a couplet from Nietzsche—from the section of rhymes that open *The Gay Science*—and concludes with a series of six written meditations.[34] Bataille admits that the meditations "cannot alone constitute an initiation into the *exercise* of a mysticism of 'joy before death.'" He goes on to specify that "these writings represent, moreover, less exercises strictly speaking than simple descriptions of a contemplative state or of an ecstatic contemplation. These descriptions would not even be acceptable if they were not given for what they are, in other words, as free. Only the very first text could be proposed as an exercise."[35]

This is the first text:

I abandon myself to peace, to the point of annihilation.

The noises of the struggle are lost in death, as rivers are lost in the sea, as stars burst in the night.
The strength of the struggle is fulfilled in the silence of all action.

I enter into peace as I enter into a dark unknown.
I fall in this dark unknown.
I myself become this dark unknown.[36]

Setting aside this text for a moment, we can observe that Bataille's point in the lines quoted above is to distinguish the experiential aspects of his practice of meditation from both the oral and written forms of that practice. The oral and written forms or modes of the practice cannot take the place of the experience itself. On this point in *Inner Experience*, he also notes that the "written tradition is hardly more than an introduction to the oral one."[37] The priority, then, is on the experience itself rather than on any spoken or written text, religious, literary, or otherwise, that might be related to it. Nevertheless, the oral and written forms accompany the experience that results from meditation in two ways: in some cases as exercises and in others as descriptions or evocations. Exercises serve to *provoke* experience. Descriptions merely reflect it. The relationship between these two modes—exercises and descriptions—is both complex and subtle. Descriptions can be a helpful crutch for the practitioner in the process of meditation. They can provide structure for the process itself, leading the practitioner ever deeper, in distinct steps, into the experience. One highly developed form of this kind of structured meditation appears in Zen Buddhism, which uses *koans*, or "public documents" presented as brief stories or dialogues on specific themes or problems, as a means of directing students through specific stages of meditational practice.[38]

Beyond these two formal modes, the meditations themselves, particularly the first one, quoted above, are also narrative or quasi-narrative in structure. Each statement contains elements of action alongside the descriptive elements: details about the journey of the individual slipping into joy before death, or what Bataille will later call inner experience. I *enter* into . . . I *fall* into . . . I *become* this dark unknown.

Stepping back slightly, we can recall that in the Christian methods of meditation that Bataille adapted into his own method of meditation, those of Ignatius de Loyola's *Spiritual Exercises* and of Saint John of the Cross in particular, the relationship between the narrative descriptions of the agony of Christ, imagined dramatic mimicry, and the practice of meditation are crucial.[39] The narrative description of Christ's suffering forms the basis of Loyola's dramatic mimicry, the imagined identification of the Christian with Christ. In *Inner Experience*, Bataille specifies, in language consistent with the meditation quoted above: "According to Saint John of the Cross, we must imitate in God (Jesus) the fall, the agony, the moment of 'nonknowledge' of the *lama sabachthani*; drunk to the lees, Christianity is the absence of salvation, the despair of God."[40] He is even more specific about the dramatic process required by the *Spiritual Exercises* of Ignatius de Loyola:

> To dramatize is what the devout people who follow the *Exercises* of Saint Ignatius do (but not them alone). If one were to imagine the place, the characters of the drama and the drama itself: the torture to which Christ is led. The disciple of Saint Ignatius offers himself a theatrical representation. He is in a peaceful room: he is asked to have the feelings he would have on Calvary. He is told that despite the peacefulness of his room, he *should* have these feelings. One desires that he should get out of himself, deliberately dramatizing this human life, of which one knows in advance that it is likely to be a half-anxious, half-dozing futility. But not yet having had a properly inner life, before having shattered discourse within him, he is asked to project the point about which I have spoken, similar to him—but even more similar to that which he wants to be—in the person of Jesus agonizing. The projection of the point, in Christianity, is attempted before the mind has its inner movements at its disposal, before it has become free of discourse. It is only the rough projection, which one attempts, starting from it, to attain non-discursive experience.[41]

In these spiritual exercises, language is used against itself, not for its own sake but toward the provocation of an experience. The words themselves form a screen that either falls away or is torn apart through meditation. The dramatic structure provided by the agony of Jesus also functions as a vehicle for the practice of meditation in such a way that it opens up, in fact cleaves into the ontological dilemma of human being. Rather than serving as an illustration of a stable idea within a systematic theology, in this mode, the peak of the dramatic narrative, crucifixion, opens onto a physically palpable space of dizzying ecstasy. Mystical meditation, in several Christian traditions, is thus profoundly distinct from systematic theology in its processes and goals even though the two modes of practice are built upon and focused on the same dramatic narrative. Systematic theology is rooted in the production of knowledge, while mysticism is rooted in lived human experience. As Jacques Lacan later observed, discussing mystic speech in Seminar XX, the "essential testimony of the mystics consists in saying that they experience it [jouissance], but know nothing about it."[42] Mystic speech isn't rooted in or even intended as a search for knowledge; it's speech that does not know or rather that knows nothing. It's speech about nothing, nothing that can be clarified with speech. Maurice Blanchot touches on the same problem when describing the distinct form of literary language that is his true country in the introduction to his first collection of critical essays, *Faux pas* (1943):

> The writer finds himself in the increasingly ludicrous condition of having nothing to write, of having no means with which to write it, and of being constrained by the utter necessity of always writing it. Having nothing to express must be taken in the most literal way. Whatever he would like to say, it is nothing. The world, things, knowledge are to him only landmarks across the void. And he himself is already reduced to nothing. Nothingness is his material. . . . [T]he "I have nothing to say" of the writer, like that of the accused, encloses the whole secret of his solitary condition.[43]

Mystic speech nevertheless can serve meditational purposes and, by extension, political and social ones as well. By standing apart from the hierarchal, indeed patriarchal speech of rationalistic and systematic theology, mystic speech provides an alternative form of political and social speech, rooted in the passions, affects, and the body. Just as mystical experience transcends political and social hierarchy—anyone can be visited by a mystical experience or vocation, the lowest peasant, the highest king, male or female—mystic speech too transcends political and social hierarchies: training in rhetoric is not required. It might even be detrimental to it. Moreover, while systematic theology may be harnessed for political purposes, to explain and thus reify, for example, power relations, mystic speech always returns to the affects and experience of the individual mystic. It may be cited but it cannot be entirely co-opted or otherwise put to use. Its meaning cannot be either summarized or consumed by its evidentiary or other uses but instead always remains tied to individual experience. It is always in some ways both before and beyond the political and the social. It is *before* these spheres because it does not meet their criteria; it is neither accomplished nor sophisticated. It is beyond them because it reveals their limits by exceeding them, by saying something that they cannot say, speaking in a way that they cannot speak.[44]

In addition to St. Ignatius de Loyola and St. John of the Cross, Bataille quotes St. Teresa of Ávila, Dionysius the Areopagite, Meister Eckhart, St. Catherine of Siena, and, perhaps most fervently, Angela of Foligno, in writings across many years, particularly beginning at the end of the 1930s. As a young man, after the First World War, the book on his bedside table had been Remy de Gourmont's *Le Latin Mystique* (1892), an anthology of one thousand years of ecclesiastic poetry in Latin, including mystic verse. Years later, writing during the first days of the Second World War, Bataille begins *Guilty* with the admission that he finds reading impossible; although, as he says, Angela of Foligno's *Book of Visions*, "grips me to the point of trembling."[45] As noted above regarding St. John of the Cross, as much as Bataille writes in the tradition of the accursed poets, he also writes in that of the great mystics, sharing their language, their metaphors, and their strategies if not necessarily their ultimate faith.

But are the meditations from "The Practice of Joy before Death" actually poems? Aside from the first one, quoted above, I have not included them in the present volume. They strike me as among the final steps Bataille took on the road to poetry rather than as purely and distinctly poetic speech. The burden they face is more insistently linked to the meditational practice of joy before death than to their own formal necessities. And, however interesting they may be to us, Bataille himself set them aside or simply moved beyond them as both his methods of meditational practice and strategies of writing developed over the next few years. As he said in *Inner Experience*, speaking specifically of the political and religious communities he attempted to forge in the late 1930s, but also in some ways to his resolutely social focus, including the focus of his writing: "The war put an end to my 'activity' and my life became all the less separated from the object of its search."[46] This is not to say that Bataille simply turned away from politics at the beginning of the war. *Guilty* begins with a related paradox: "The date I begin writing (5 September 1939) is not a coincidence. I begin because of the events, but not to speak of them."[47] The events in question were the events that signaled the beginning of World War II.

The first writings by Bataille that can be both identified as poems and reliably dated appear in the "Torture" section of *Inner Experience*, which he wrote two years later during the fall and winter of 1941. Additional poems appear elsewhere in that book, including in the fifth and final section, which, though brief, consists entirely of poetry. He completed the manuscript of *Inner Experience* over the summer of 1942 but he did not stop writing or stop writing poems. Quite the contrary in fact, Bataille wrote perhaps the most substantial number of his poems during the fall of 1942. On medical leave from his job at the Bibliothèque nationale, he was living in the relative isolation of Panilleuse, a small village in Normandy. There he wrote portions of *Guilty*, *The Little One*, *The Dead Man*, *The Accursed Share*, and *The Oresteia*, as well as other unfinished works, notes, drafts, and sketches, including many of the poems in this volume. The body of poetry Bataille wrote that fall formed a kind of crucible and archive of his work, particularly his work as a poet, over the next few years. Over those years, through 1945 and beyond, Bataille would return to the archive of verse written during the fall of 1942 to find poems that he would then rework and, more importantly rearrange or reassemble, in new combinations and for new contexts of publication.

The poems included in *The Oresteia* represent only the most dramatic example of this process. Written alongside the other works that fall, Bataille published three sections of the work independently in journals in 1943 and 1945. He reedited those sections for inclusion in *The Oresteia* when he published it as a separate volume in 1945 and again when he brought it together with *A Story of Rats* and *Dianus* for publication as *The Hatred of Poetry* in 1947. He reworked them again, though less substantially, when he republished *The Hatred of Poetry* under a new title, *The Impossible*, in 1962. The three sections initially published on their own in journals appeared in those venues as independent but contiguous entities. For inclusion in *The Oresteia*, Bataille broke each section apart into a number of shorter poems, giving each smaller section its own page. Several sections of two of these three works were also eliminated or relocated elsewhere in the final version of the work.[48]

Bataille also used poems written during the fall of 1942 in a work that remained unpublished, *The Tomb of Louis XXX*, and gathered others into several separate folders within the archive he organized—as a good librarian—of his own manuscripts. Because Bataille revisited and reworked these poems so frequently over the subsequent years, it is extremely difficult to date the works accurately, let alone arrange them chronologically in order of their composition.

Bataille also continued writing poems throughout this period. Additional poems appear in the manuscripts and notes for *Guilty*, completed in spring and summer of 1943. During the late summer and fall of that year, however, Bataille wrote his most sustained body of verse, from which he published a section that fall, and then later, the following year, as a complete work under the title *Archangelic*. Additional poems figure in the manuscripts for *On Nietzsche*, written during the spring of 1944. But following the liberation of Paris in August 1944 and the end of the war the next spring, poetry again receded for several years as a privileged form of writing for Bataille. He would not return to writing poetry until 1954, when he wrote a relatively large number of poems and selected a few of them for publication in *Botteghe oscure* under the collective title, *Undifferentiated Being Is Nothing*. He wrote his final poems three years later, in 1957, the year that saw the publication, through three different publishers, of three distinct and distinctly significant major works, his novel *Blue of Noon*, his sociological study *Eroticism*, and his collection of literary criticism, *Literature and Evil*. Perhaps poetry reappeared at that moment as a reflection and extension of this range of writings.

This series of dates can be summarized with the observation that Bataille wrote poetry in more or less contained periods, even in bursts of creative activity, and indeed that he wrote the majority of his poetry from 1942 to 1945, which is to say not only during the war but, more importantly, during the period of the Nazi occupation of France. The seeds of that writing may have been planted in the context of and influences upon his work prior to the war, as well as in the models and practices of meditation he developed in the late 1930s, but they did not sprout until the period of the war itself, and indeed more specifically that of the Nazi occupation. Moreover, since Bataille's recourse to verse substantially receded with the end of the war, we can link that mode of literary production rather more directly to that specific period of his life as well as to the horizon of meaning bounded by those conditions. Linking this observation back to the role of the accursed poet, we can also say that it is one thing for literature to plead guilty and yet another for it to do so under conditions of enemy occupation.

But Bataille was hardly alone in this endeavor. A few months after the end of the occupation, in October 1944, the provisional government hosted a gala celebration, attended by Charles de Gaulle, then acting president of the republic, to celebrate the "Poets of the Resistance." In his opening statement, François Mauriac observed: "There have never been so many poets as during these dark years."[49] In many cases, the dense metaphors, allusions, and abstractions of poetic language permitted poems to pass under the red pen of the censors without remark. Whether such oversights testify to a love of poetry, a failure of comprehension, or cultural chagrin is hard to say. They also testify to the challenge faced by poets in crafting consequential verse. If the censors fail to notice the inherent threat posed by the words on the page, perhaps those words have missed their mark.

In Bataille's case, the venues in which he published his poetry directly reflect the wartime conditions of its composition, and more than that, his place within a wide group of writers who viewed literary writing, and poetry specifically, as means of political resistance. Bataille's first published poems appeared within the text of *Inner Experience*, released by Éditions Gallimard in February 1943. But later that same year, he also published two poems, or perhaps rather two groups of poems, in an anthology volume entitled *Domaine Français*. One of these groups of poems, entitled "La Douleur" (Pain) would later be republished under the title "Le Tombeau" (The Tomb) as the first part of *Archangelic*. The other was "Invocation à la chance" (The Invocation of Chance), which would later be published as the first few poems of *The Oresteia*. Taken together these pieces represent selections from Bataille's two major collections of poetry.

Domaine Français was published in partnership by Éditions Messages, Paris, and Éditions Trois-Collines, Geneva. Jean Lescure edited the collection from Paris but it had to be published in neutral Switzerland due to censorship imposed by the Nazi occupation. Lescure cofounded Éditions Messages in 1937 as a venue intending to explore the range and purpose of poetic writing, particularly at the intersections of poetry, philosophy, and the visual arts, in what turned out to be the final days of peace. After a small initial publication, the first true issue of the journal appeared in 1939. It was devoted to William Blake. The issue included texts by Lescure, Jean Wahl, Herbert Read, and others as well as some translations of Blake's works. A second issue appeared that same year, gathering texts by philosophers and poets Jean Wahl, Gaston Bachelard, Paul Éluard, T. S. Eliot, and others under the heading of poetry and metaphysics. The beginning of the war refocused and deepened Lescure's purposes for the journal. It already had something it stood for—poetry, philosophy, and French civilization—now it also had something to stand against.

The Nazi occupation of France in June 1940 was at once military, political, and cultural. Jewish and Communist writers and artists were, for example, banned from publishing and exhibiting well before they were marked for deportation. The occupiers also demanded that key administrative posts in cultural institutions of all kinds be filled with writers and artists sympathetic to their goals. Perhaps the most famous instance of this involved the editorship of the *La Nouvelle Revue Française*. Founded in 1909 as the nucleus of what became Éditions Gallimard, the *NRF* was the premiere literary and cultural journal in France for thirty years. Publication was suspended for several months at the beginning of the occupation, but in December of 1940, Gaston Gallimard capitulated with the demands of the new regime by replacing the long-time editor of the *NRF*, Jean Paulhan, with a Nazi sympathizer, Pierre Drieu la Rochelle.

Publishing in France, in the *NRF* and otherwise, became a political act. Some writers simply continued to publish: eventually many of them would be viewed as collaborators with the Nazi regime and face consequences including exile and even execution after the war. Others, like the poet René Char, chose not to publish in France until the occupation had ended. Char took up arms and joined a resistance cell in his native Provence. Still other writers began working for an underground press that slowly took root and began to spread throughout the occupied and Vichy controlled zones of the country. Many pursued several of these strategies simultaneously. Albert Camus, for example, published books with Gallimard during the occupation but he also became the editor of the important underground newspaper *Combat*.

In this context, facing these choices, Jean Lescure reinvented Éditions Messages as a vehicle of resistance. It would be quasi-clandestine: the authors would sign their texts with their own names rather than with pseudonyms but the publication dates would frequently be falsified, suggesting that the individual issues of the journal had been printed prior to various edicts imposed by the occupying regime. Eventually, Lescure would also begin to work with printers in Belgium and Switzerland, as he did for *Domaine Français*, as another means of avoiding censorship.

Lescure did not intend to publish political propaganda or censored news. *Messages* was a literary journal first and foremost. Propaganda, he believed, put literature in service to a cause and therefore drained it of its primary, literary value. Put differently, polemic, no matter how vigorous, is almost always ultimately dull and easily dismissed, once one understands the perspective it intends to serve. If *Messages* intended to take a stand *against* the Nazi occupiers, it would have to do so indirectly, or from a perspective beyond or distinct from direct opposition.

Toward this end in *Messages*, Lescure hoped to explore the relationship between poetry and liberty at its most basic level, that of language. "Resistance," he later wrote, "began with language. . . . We took upon ourselves the charge of making the French language live. We became aware, passionately, of what it is to speak a language. We discovered the deep existence in us of this French language that had been formed over centuries, in the words and forms of which without us realizing it, everything of our lives was stated, in which we had discovered the world and ourselves."[50] Under conditions of enemy occupation, even speaking one's own language constitutes an act of resistance.[51] For Lescure and his collaborators, the French language became, once more, a heritage of expressions and ideas bound together and, more importantly, a force of community. As Lescure began to reformulate *Messages* as a journal of resistance, he realized that the core focus of the journal would be poetry: "It was poetry that I wanted to bring to light this time, more than philosophy. Poetry appeared to me as the first image of freedom. Philosophy, though it could be the discourse of that freedom, did not live freedom as immediately."[52] Philosophy, in other words, can speak about freedom but it cannot speak freely. It cannot surrender itself to the intense emotions and vivacity of human experience the way that poetry, in this conception of poetry, can. Bataille, for his part, would say much the same thing a decade later: "[P]hilosophy in so far as it is a specialized undertaking is work. That is to say that it excludes without even deigning to notice them . . . moments of intense emotion."[53] The language of philosophy is the language of servitude, while that of poetry is freedom.

As this orientation began to become known—through quiet whispers spoken behind safely closed doors—a very loose community of poets, writers, and artists began to form around *Messages*. Motivated in no small part by his dismissal from the *NRF*, Jean Paulhan played an instrumental role in expanding Lescure's community of collaborators, reaching out in particular to authors associated with Gallimard. *Messages* became a self-conscious and socially recognized alternative to the Nazi sanctioned *NRF*. It did not, however, hope to become or represent a coherently organized group or movement: that too would have been to put poetry in service to something other than language itself. "On the one hand, we did not cease for one moment from feeling ourselves to be engaged in a war against Nazism, on the other we refused to enslave poetry to one of the discourses whose propaganda had made us mute."[54] (Communists in France had, for example, been silent for the first year of the occupation out of allegiance to the Soviet Union, which did not declare war on Germany until the Germans broke the non-aggression pact that bound the two countries in 1942.)

Bataille's first contribution to the journal, "Nietzsche's Laughter," appeared in a 1942 issue entitled *Exercise du Silence*, a phrase pregnant with meaning not only in the paradox of poetry but also in an occupied country subjected to censorship laws and curfews.[55] Printed in Belgium in hopes of avoiding some of the problems of censorship, the issue opened with a quotation from St. John of the Cross and, in addition to Bataille's essay, also included contributions by Lescure, Paul Éluard, Raymond Queneau, Michel Leiris, Roger Gilbert-Lecomte, Jean Tardieu, Arthur Adamov, Michel Fardoulis-Lagrange, Michel Carrouges, Gaston Bachelard, and Jean-Paul Sartre, as well as archival documents from Charles Baudelaire and Alfred Jarry. Significantly, within this list we find the names of several individuals who were participating that year in a reading group organized by Bataille under the aegis of a Collège socratique (Socratic College): Jean Lescure, Michel Leiris, Raymond Queneau, and Michel Fardoulis-Lagrange. Another member of the group, Raoul Ubac, collaborated on other issues of *Messages*. Maurice Blanchot participated in the group but did not publish in *Messages* and, moreover, did not write poetry.[56] Bataille believed the group had the purpose of discussing inner experience: he was then writing the book that would take that phrase as its title. Lescure believed their purpose had been to discuss Nietzsche: he described "Nietzsche's Laughter" as an extract from these proceedings.[57]

Bataille's first contribution to *Messages* had been philosophical prose, "Nietzsche's Laughter." His second, as noted, was poetry: sections of both *Archangelic* and *The Oresteia* in the anthology volume *Domaine Français* in August 1943. The 450-

page collection gathered together many of the most prominent names in French literature: André Gide, Paul Valéry, Romain Rolland, Paul Claudel, Gaston Bachelard, Benjamin Fondane, Julien Benda, Paul Éluard, Philippe Soupault, Louis Aragon, Pierre Jean Jouve, Albert Camus, Jean-Paul Sartre, Henri Michaux, Jean Paulhan, Raymond Queneau, Francis Ponge, Michel Fardoulis-Lagrange, Jean Lescure, Michel Leiris, as well as Bataille. Over the next year and a half, Bataille also published several essays in the underground newspaper *Combat*, and, as the war came to an end, cofounded his own short-lived political journal, *Actualité*. In that final year of the war, Bataille published more poetry in Paul Éluard's politically oriented literary journal *L'Éternelle Revue* and in Henri Parisot's *Quatre vents*, which also published *The Oresteia* as a separate volume. Two years later, in 1947, Bataille republished *The Oresteia* along with two new texts, *A Story of Rats* and *Dianus*, under the title *The Hatred of Poetry*. The collection was published by Éditions de Minuit, perhaps *the* quintessential press of the resistance in France, founded for the purpose of publishing underground writing during the occupation.[58] *Le Silence de la Mer* (The Silence of the Sea, 1942) by Jean Bruller, writing under the pseudonym Vercors, had been its inaugural publication.

My point here is to suggest that we should read Bataille's work from the period of the occupation, and his poetry in particular, in light of the goals and ambitions that shaped and animated not only *Messages* but also several other organs of underground and resistance writing. Bataille, it seems, did not begin writing poetry until the occupation, possibly not even until he had come in contact with Jean Lescure and Lescure's conception of poetry and poetic language as a mode and means of freedom and consequently political resistance. This is not to say that Bataille rigidly or even entirely subscribed to Lescure's views or, for that matter, that Lescure became simply another disciple of Bataille's. Lescure himself admits that Bataille had a tremendous "power of attraction" and that he could possibly have taken charge of *Messages*, as he had *Documents* and *Acéphale*. But, he also says that, in this case, Bataille "contented himself with finding among us accomplices to share his appetite for research."[59] The question of Bataille's subordination to Lescure or Lescure's subordination to Bataille obscures the paradox of poetic resistance that, in some ways, brought them together. But what is it, exactly, to fight for freedom through poetry?

In *On Nietzsche*, another book written in explicit acknowledgment of the conditions of enemy occupation, Bataille addressed the paradox of resistance in relation to the problem of subordination. His language here is distinctly Hegelian, recalling the paradox of the master-slave dialectic, in which the master is never more than the slave of the slave, the freedom fighter always subordinate to the oppressor:

> Life remains whole only by not being subordinated to some specific object that surpasses it. In this sense, totality has freedom as its essence. Nevertheless I cannot want to become a whole man by the simple fact of fighting for freedom. Even if fighting in this way is the activity among all others appropriate to me, I could not confuse, within myself, the state of integrity and my fighting. It is the positive exercise of freedom, not the negative struggle against a particular oppression, that elevates me above mutilated existence. Each of us learns bitterly that fighting for his freedom is first of all alienating.[60]

Later in the same passage, he brought his conclusions into line with the problems of good and evil, which is to say, of the accursed poets: "I've said the exercise of freedom is situated on the side of evil, while the struggle for freedom is the conquest of a *good*. If life is whole in me, to the extent that it is, I cannot put it in service to some good, whether that of someone else or of God or myself, without dividing it up."[61] The paradox of poetic resistance involves writing in such a way as to demonstrate and indeed experience a positive freedom through writing without, however, surrendering that freedom to service for a cause, even if that cause is the idea of freedom. This challenge also recalls Bataille's formulation of the experience of inner experience: "Inner experience cannot have its principle in a dogma (a moral attitude), in a science (knowledge cannot be either its goal or its origin), or in a search for enriching states (the aesthetic, experimental attitude), it cannot have any other concern or other goal than itself."[62] Blanchot is similarly succinct on this topic: "How could poetry, if one sees in it the soul's supreme act of power, allow itself to rely on a pre-established religious certainty, on a dogmatic intuition with which it is supposed to be content?"[63]

Bataille's most direct statements about the specific mechanisms of poetry appear in *Inner Experience*:

> When words like horse or butter enter into a poem, they do so detached from interested concerns. For as many times as the words butter and horse are put to practical ends, the use that poetry makes of them liberates human life from these ends. When the farm girl says butter or the stable boy says horse, they know butter, horse. The knowledge that they have of them even in a sense exhausts the idea of knowing, for they can make butter or lead a horse at will. . . . But, on the contrary, poetry leads from the known to the unknown. It can do what neither the boy nor the girl can do, introduce a butter horse. In this way it places one before the unknowable. No doubt I have barely enunciated the words when the familiar images of horses and butter present themselves, but they are solicited only in order to die. In this poetry is sacrifice, the most accessible sacrifice. For if the use or abuse of words, to which

the operations of work oblige us, takes place on the ideal, unreal level of language, the same is true of the sacrifice of words that is poetry.[64]

Poetry, in other words, is a mode of speech in which words are separated from their direct, common, and useful meanings. Words become unmoored, are set adrift in a sea of signification. Unexpected meanings may be revealed or created, whether through the internal resources of language, etymologies, or through the surprising juxtaposition of words or phrases. The point to poetry, to writing poetry, for Bataille, consists primarily in this act of separation, of severing, that splits words from expected meanings, from common use. Poetry does violence to language, to meaning, to the structures of language that support meaning; this is also to say, more broadly, that support meaning in human life. Poetry raises questions about the processes and possibilities of meaning in human life, about the ways that human beings create meaning in the world. In poetry, meaning becomes a problem or question in language. The above-quoted passage from *Inner Experience* began still more forcefully:

> Of poetry, I will now say that it is, I believe, the sacrifice in which words are victims. Words—we use them, we make of them the instruments of useful acts. We wouldn't be human if language within us had to be entirely servile. Nor can we do with the efficacious relationships that words introduce between men and things. But we tear words from these relationships in a delirium.[65]

It is significant to note that this interpretation of the mechanisms of poetic speech places emphasis on the event of that speech rather than on any lasting results that may be derived from it. If poetry liberates previously unknown structures and possibilities for meaning in language, the repetition of those structures is no longer, strictly speaking, poetry. As he puts it in *Guilty*: "[P]oetry that is not engaged in an experience exceeding poetry (distinct from it) is not the movement but the residue left by the turbulence."[66] However beautiful, however apt, the repetition of poetic figures, phrases, or combinations of words is, for Bataille, mere literature. This ambivalence in his thought is occasionally difficult to follow. All too frequently the word literature seems to indicate a positive good; or the words poetry and literature might be used almost interchangeably. But when he is speaking specifically, trying to be precise, literature indicates a degraded form of poetic language—"mere literature"—while poetry indicates another kind of experience altogether. Literature is a mode of discourse, like science, philosophy, or theology; whereas poetry partakes of the sacred, of the violence of the sacred. Poetry lives in the moment, literature aspires for the ages.

For Bataille, the poetic act is a violent act and a sacrificial one, an act wherein the stability of meaning is sacrificed. Poetry does not allow meaning to accrete, to gather richness, nuance, or the careful certainty of familiar and stable linguistic constructions. Poetry puts meaning in suspense, sets words teetering on the edge of the unknown, on nonsense, on the void. Thus poets do not contribute to the sum of knowledge: they demonstrate its frailty, the extent to which discursive knowledge is dependent on the ultimately arbitrary affiliation of words and meanings. Poetry preys upon and reveals the mortality of words.

The sacrifice of meaning sets words free. In poetry, words are free of expected meanings, free of utility. This is one paradox of free speech. In contemporary political discourse, the phrase free speech too often suggests the mere freedom of the individual to say whatever he or she may wish to say, to simply express an opinion, whether wise, daft, unfounded, or reprehensible. For Bataille, however, the freedom to express this or that opinion is not truly freedom at all. It's repetition: the freedom to repeat or represent an opinion, whether received via tradition or personally conceived, and now congealed. In Bataille's conception, on the other hand, poetry allows the individual to participate in the freedom of speech to traverse and transgress unexpected, even impossible meanings. The difference here is between speaking freely and freeing speech.

Freedom of speech, for Bataille, is *prior* to subjective opinion or expression. By setting words free in poetry, the poet explores the possibility and impossibility of meaning itself, potentially discovering possibilities of meaning as well as the limits of those possibilities. Moreover, as Bataille insists, "poetry is not self-understanding, still less the experience of the most distant possible (of that which, previously didn't exist) but the evocation through words of this experience."[67] The emphasis, for Bataille, remains firmly on experience rather than expression. And this can of course be a humbling and terrifying experience, though it is a fundamentally liberating one that can also provoke laughter. To write, as Bataille says in *The Little One*, "is to research chance."[68] Poetry, in other words, partakes of a fundamental freedom, not simply to *say* whatever one wants to say, to repeat received wisdom, but rather to explore the possibility and impossibility of what might be said.

Within these structures, what Bataille calls the hatred of poetry is an active principle; it is hatred motivated to actively erode language, to destroy the capacity of words to mean something, to represent something. Poetry ruins, destroys, or disintegrates language. The hatred of poetry—the hatred that poetic language brings into the world—is also the hatred of the limited meaning of words, of narrowly discursive language, of words stuck in discourses, disciplines, even languages. Needless to say, the capacity of poetic language, the capacity of words to split off from narrow definitions, to mean more than one thing, is one aspect of poetic language that some readers hate. Readers in search of information and stable structures of meaning and reference often find the slippery playfulness and variability of poetic language—indeed, occasionally the dizziness and delirium of poetic language—intolerable.

The hatred of poetry, the hatred that *is* poetry, is evil. It's evil in the sense that it disrupts the *good* use of language, the utility and stability, the reliability of language. It disrupts the rules that govern speech. Pushing this interpretation to its limits, poetry, Bataille claims, is "outside the law."[69] This law is the law of speech, grammar, but it is also paradoxically both the law of nature and the law of culture. The human being is the being that is a problem in nature, the being that raises a question about nature, about its own nature and is place in nature. As Bataille puts it: "The heart is human to the extent that it rebels. Not being a beast, but a man, signifies refusing the law (that of nature)."[70] Or again, more forcefully, in *Guilty*: "The human condition is, strictly speaking, reducible to the contestation of nature by itself (to the interrogation of being by itself)."[71] This rebellion is ultimately also a rebellion against culture, against the law that is culture as well. Culture consists in the codification of our human rebellion against nature: a set of norms—however variant through time and place—defining acceptable responses to our condition, necessarily variable in time and place. The violence of poetry violates these norms as well, and necessarily so. Culture may be a necessary support system for human life, but that is not to say that challenging that support system is not equally necessary. This paradox is at the center of Bataille's thought. As he puts it: "[E]ach man must be useful to his fellows, but he is their enemy if there is nothing in him beyond utility."[72] This is also another way of thinking about the paradox of poetry as a mode of political resistance. Speech that is political in a direct way, that aspires to be politically useful, is not free speech. It is journalism, propaganda, or perhaps even literature, in Bataille's derogatory sense of that term, mere literature, merely beautiful words or phrases. Poetry—words set free—fulfills, on the other hand, a politics beyond utility by demonstrating the essence of freedom not as an idea but as an event.

Writing within this theoretical framework, Bataille wrote several distinct kinds of poems. Some of his poems tend toward lyrical expressiveness. The poems of *Archangelic* offer an example of this type. Other poems push the meanings of individual words or phrases to an anti-discursive extreme. Still others fall more closely into line with Bataille's methods of meditation, sketching the steps of consciousness in meditational practice. Occasionally all of these strategies are present in a single poem.

Not all of the poetry collected here, it should be said, is equally successful. More than half of it remained unpublished at the time of Bataille's death. The successive drafts he devoted to various poems testify to the instability of his search for poetry. Reading the notes for this volume, one can, I think, sense Bataille trying words in different and distinct combinations, searching for effects, for ruptures in discourse, in other words, for poetry.

Most often, Bataille's poetry deploys words, scenes, landscapes, and figures that one finds in his fictions and in his autobiographical prose. Here they are heightened, set apart, pushed to extremes, to the breaking point of contradiction, where meaning becomes elusive or slips away entirely, where sense becomes nonsense. Many of Bataille's poems, born of mystic speech, border on incantation, set on drone, draining words of meaning. If they are repetitive, even boring, it is often to this purpose. As noted, these poems don't aspire to gather or reinforce meaning, they shed it, strip it away.

Figures familiar from Bataille's other writings reappear here, all but utterly stripped of context: the blind man, who might evoke Bataille's father, blind at the end of his life; the dead woman, who might evoke Laure, who died in the bed they shared, or Bataille's mother, whose corpse he evokes on other notable occasions in his work. Scenes, landscapes provide the armature, the root of place even as they are drained of uniqueness or specificity through repetition or compression. Autobiography, if that's what this is, tips over into fiction, or psychological fantasy.

Many of these poems are also explicitly erotic or, rather, erotic in very explicit ways. This is unsurprising from the author of *Story of the Eye* and *Madame Edwarda*, but one should be careful to note which of these poems Bataille published and which he did not. Many of the most scabrous texts went unpublished during his lifetime. A few were intended for publication, like *Story of the Eye* and *Madame Edwarda*, under pseudonyms or in small, limited, or private editions. Bataille's erotic writing, in short, was often clandestine writing of a completely different sort than the underground writing of political resistance. Closer to the eroticism of these poems is perhaps that of Bataille's *The Little One* (1943) or *Alleluia: The Catechism of Dianus* (written 1944, published 1947), both semi- or pseudo-autobiographical erotic meditations rather than fictional narratives.

All in all, Bataille's poetry, perhaps more so than any of his other modes of writing, should be understood in light of the context that shaped its composition and publication, which is to say, in light of the Nazi occupation of France and the psychological, social, and political crises occasioned by the occupation. *Inner Experience*, *Guilty*, *On Nietzsche*, and *The Oresteia* date to the same period and each include poetry. Yet Bataille's earliest plans for a collective edition of these works proposed bringing them together under the title "Beyond Poetry."[73] Reflecting on this title in light of the theory of poetry outlined above, we should remember that, for Bataille, all real poetry is, strictly speaking, beyond poetry. He said as much in a 1946 review article about Jacques Prévert: "Jacques Prévert's poetry is poetry precisely as a living denial—and derision—of whatever congeals the mind in the name of poetry itself. . . . For what *is* poetry is also the actuality, in the life of poetry, which is the derision of poetry."[74] Prévert's poetry, he said, is "poetry because, in itself, it harshly effects the ruin of poetry."[75]

Given the consistency and depth of these views, the extent of Bataille's exploration of them both in theory and in practice, and their central place in his ideas about inner experience and writing in these years, why did Bataille stop writing poetry?

The end of the war provides part of an answer. If poetry was a distinct mode of political speech during the war, if pleading guilty was a mode of freedom under conditions of enemy occupation, the end of the war lent a new necessity to other modes of political speech. Already in early 1945—months after the liberation of Paris but months before the end of the war—Bataille began planning a new series of publications on political topics under the title *Actualité* (Current Events), though only the first volume in the series—on Spain—was to appear. By the end of the year, he had cofounded the journal *Critique*. In the immediate postwar period, Bataille's writing, in other words, was otherwise engaged.

Another part of an answer might also be glimpsed through the variety and volume of Bataille's literary and critical endeavors in the immediate aftermath of the war. One reason he wrote so much was that he needed the money. Bataille had been living on a small stipend contingent on medical leave from his position at the Bibliothèque nationale since 1942. That stipend was discontinued in September 1946. It had never really been sufficient. The extraordinary range of Bataille's literary experimentation in this moment coincided, I think unsurprisingly, with his pressing financial need. During the final year of the war and in its immediate aftermath, Bataille wrote *On Nietzsche, Alleluia: The Catechism of Dianus, The Oresteia, Memorandum, Method of Meditation, The Story of Rats, Dianus, The Tomb of Louis XXX*, a screenplay, a play for radio, and essays for several journals, as well as founding two journals, *Actualité* and *Critique*. He also continued working on *The Accursed Share*. His letters to his editors at Gallimard frequently referenced the possible financial viability of his projects.[76] Thus while he may have disdained the art market in his prewar article, "The Sacred," as we saw earlier, in the postwar period he could no longer afford to do so. In this moment, his energies shifted away from poetry toward longer, more financially viable forms, including long-form critical essays and the novel.

But this shift in Bataille's literary output also had roots in his ambivalence toward poetry as a form and toward traditional, literary poetry—beautiful words—in particular. Already in *Inner Experience*, he observed: "The one who sacrifices, the poet, having unceasingly to bring ruin into the ungraspable world of words, quickly tires of enriching a literary treasure. He is condemned to it: if he lost the taste for treasure, he would cease to be a poet."[77] In context, the phrase "literary treasure" refers to surrealism, but it is also more broadly applicable. The poet may feel compelled to write—as Bataille was—out of a need for the experience of freedom that writing provides. But the poet may also be compelled to write out of the love of literature, out of the psychological need to contribute to the store of literary treasure. In Bataille's view, that treasure can lose its luster all too easily. Ultimately though, words are empty husks, literature is mere literature, and the poet comes to realize that, as Bataille puts it in *Inner Experience*, "what counts is not the statement of the wind, it's the wind."[78]

As noted above, in *Method of Meditation*, written in 1945 and 1946, Bataille praised poetry as a sovereign behavior: a means of attaining freedom, however briefly. By the following year, however, he had already begun to temper that enthusiasm. In his review of Jean-Paul Sartre's introduction to the intimate writings of Charles Baudelaire, Bataille clearly perceived the limits of poetry as a form and as a mode of political speech. He wrote:

> If liberty . . . is the essential quality of poetry, and if free and sovereign behavior deserves no more than a 'tortured quest,' the misery of poetry and the bonds imposed by liberty become evident. Though poetry

may trample verbally on the established order, it is no substitute for it. When disgust with a powerless liberty thoroughly commits the poet to political action he abandons poetry. . . . Poetic existence, in which we once saw the possibility of a sovereign attitude, is really a minor attitude. It becomes no more than a child's attitude, a gratuitous game.[79]

The final phrase of this quotation is equivocal. For Bataille, the gratuitous game played by the child is a positive thing. Sovereignty may be a minor attitude but that too is a positive thing. The "major" attitude is that of the master, and that is the one to be scorned: the master is never more than the slave of the slave. But nevertheless within this diagnosis there is also a move, a step taken back from the praise of poetry found in Bataille's earlier discussions of the practice. Having lost whatever taste he may have briefly had for this type of literary treasure, and with political and financial necessity compelling more direct modes of writing, after the end of the war Bataille abandoned poetry for almost a decade and then returned to it only on two brief occasions, in 1954 and 1957, during which he wrote a scattering of short poems.

The abandonment of poetry haunted Bataille's reflections on the form from the very beginning. It is not insignificant, on this point, that Arthur Rimbaud consistently remained the central figure of Bataille's reflections on poetry. In Bataille's view, as he wrote: "[T]he greatness of Rimbaud is having led poetry to the failure of poetry."[80] Rimbaud pushed the experience of poetry, the freedom of poetry, to the extreme limit of poetry, and beyond, to the failure of poetry. For Rimbaud, following Bataille, the experience of the extreme took precedence over poetry itself. In the end, he abandoned poetry: "The last known poem by Rimbaud is not the extremity. If Rimbaud attained the extremity, he only attained the communication of it by means of his despair: he suppressed possible communication, he no longer wrote poems."[81]

Just as poetry cannot serve a master, a dogma, or a discipline, it also cannot serve poetry itself. If it does, it is mere literature. Poetry, for Bataille, is rebellion: against nature, against consciousness, against culture, and, not least, against literature, even against poetry. But as such, poetry is difficult, the will to write it difficult to maintain or renew. Other sovereign behaviors beckon: intoxication, eroticism, meditation, sacrifice. Words, ultimately, fail. Already in *Inner Experience*, Bataille lamented: "If man must reach the extremity, his reason collapse, *God die*, words, their sickest games, cannot suffice."[82] Being beyond poetry may also require letting poetry go, remembering that poetry matters only to the extent that it offers its writer and reader alike an experience of the impossible. And yet, paradoxically, beyond poetry there is nothing.

NOTES

1. Some critical engagements with Bataille's poetry include Marie-Christine Lala, "The Hatred of Poetry in Georges Bataille's Writing and Thought," *Bataille: Writing the Sacred*, ed. Carolyn Bailey Gill, Warwick Studies in European Thought (Routledge, 1995), pp. 105–16; Jacques Chatain, *Georges Bataille*, Poètes d'aujourd'hui (Seghers, 1973); Jacques Cels, *L'Exigence poétique de Georges Bataille* (Éditions universitaires/De Boeck, 1989); Sylvain Santi, *Georges Bataille, à l'extrémité fuyante de la poésie* (Rodopi, 2007); Marie-Christine Lala, *Georges Bataille: Poète du réel* (Peter Lang, 2010); and Jean Dragon, *La Promesse de la disparition: L'Impossible poétique de Georges Bataille* (Presses académiques francophones, 2013). A previous volume of Bataille's poetry appeared in English some twenty years ago: see Georges Bataille, *The Collected Poems of Georges Bataille*, trans. Mark Spitzer (Dufour Editions, 1998). For an appraisal of that volume, see my review in *SubStance* 92 (2000), pp. 101–04.

2. The present volume collects all of Bataille's poetry, published and unpublished, except for the poems from *The Impossible*. Regrettably, Éditions de Minuit did not grant us permission to include those poems in this volume. They are, however, available in English in Bataille, *The Impossible*, trans. Robert Hurley (1962; City Lights Books, 1991).

3. Bataille, *Inner Experience*, trans. Stuart Kendall (1943; State University of New York Press, 2014), p. 3.

4. Bataille, *The Impossible*, p. 10.

5. Bataille, *Oeuvres complètes*, vol. 3 (Gallimard, 1971), p. 512.

6. See, for example, *Method of Meditation*, in Bataille, *Inner Experience*, p. 194.

7. See Bataille, *Choix de lettres: 1917–1962*, ed. Michel Surya (Gallimard, 1997), pp. 7–8. For context, see Stuart Kendall, *Georges Bataille*, Critical Lives (Reaktion Books, 2007), p. 24.

8. For a representative selection of these essays in English, see Bataille, *Visions of Excess: Selected Writings, 1927–1939*, ed. and trans. Allan Stoekl (University of Minnesota Press, 1985).

9. See Laure, *The Collected Writings*, trans. Jeanine Herman (City Lights Books, 1995).

10. Bataille, *On Nietzsche*, trans. Stuart Kendall (1945; State University of New York Press, 2015), pp. 19, 24. This quotation brings together two quotes.

11. Bataille, *Inner Experience*, p. 3.

12. For a collected edition of Nietzsche's poetry in English, see Friedrich Nietzsche, *The Peacock and the Buffalo: The Poetry of Nietzsche*, 2nd ed., trans. James Luchte (Continuum, 2010).

13. Bataille, *Inner Experience*, p. 57. On December 8, 1941, Bataille borrowed Jean Baruzi's *Saint Jean de la Croix et le problème de l'expérience mystique* (Alcan, 1924) and Saint Jean de la Croix, *Aphorismes* (Feret, 1924) from the Bibliothèque nationale. He returned the first book on May 8, 1942, and the second on March 22, 1943. See Bataille, *Oeuvres complètes*, vol. 12 (Gallimard, 1988), p. 617.

14. Bataille came to know Jacques Prévert during the 1930s, when his first wife, the actress Sylvia Bataille, played roles in several films written by the poet. Bataille came to know René Char after World War II.

15. My purpose here is to think about influences on Bataille's poetry and poetic language. If we were considering Bataille's thought more generally, the list would shift dramatically to include the works of the Marquis de Sade, Hegel, Mauss, and Freud.

16. The other writers considered in the book are the historian Jules Michelet, the novelist (and later playwright) Jean Genet, and the Marquis de Sade. See Bataille, *Literature and Evil*, trans. Alastair Hamilton (1957; Marion Boyars, 1973).

17. Bataille, *Guilty*, trans. Stuart Kendall (1944; State University of New York Press, 2011), p. 80.

18. Bataille, *Guilty*, p. 39.

19. Bataille, *Literature and Evil*, p. xi; translation modified.

20. Bataille, "Être Oreste" (notes from 1945), *Romans et récits*, Bibliothèque de la Pléaide (Gallimard, 2004), p. 581. The word in brackets is largely illegible and therefore conjectural. On Bataille's reading of Lautréamont, see Marina Galletti, "Le Chapitre manquant de *La Littérature et le mal*: Lautréamont," *Georges Bataille, cinquante ans après*, ed. Gilles Ernst and Jean-François Louette (Éditions nouvelles Cécile Defaut, 2013), pp. 81–96.

21. Bataille, *Literature and Evil*, p. 15.

22. Bataille, *Literature and Evil*, p. 79.

23. William Blake, *The Marriage of Heaven and Hell*, pls. 3, 4.

24. Blake, *Marriage*, pl. 6.

25. Bataille, *Literature and Evil*, p. x.

26. Bataille, *Literature and Evil*, p. ix.

27. See Antonin Artaud, *Selected Writings*, ed. Susan Sontag, trans. Helen Weaver (University of California Press, 1988), pp. 452, 470, 473, 477, 486, 510.

28. Bataille, *On Nietzsche*, p. 7.

29. Bataille, *Literature and Evil*, p. ix.

30. Bataille, *On Nietzsche*, p. 8.

31. See Bataille's review of three volumes of poems by André Breton, Tristan Tzara, and Paul Éluard, *La Critique Sociale* 7 (1933), pp. 49–50; reprinted in Bataille, *Oeuvres complètes*, vol. 1 (Gallimard, 2001), pp. 323–25.

32. Bataille, "The Sacred" (1939), *Visions of Excess*, p. 245.

33. Bataille, "The Sacred," p. 240.

34. The format of the couplet in Bataille, *Visions of Excess*, makes it look like an aphorism rather than the concluding lines of a poem. For the poem in its original form and context, see Friedrich Nietzsche, *The Gay Science*, trans. Walter Kaufmann (1882; Vintage, 1974), p. 45.

35. Bataille, "The Practice of Joy before Death" (1939), *Visions of Excess*, p. 236.

36. Bataille, "Practice," p. 237.

37. Bataille, *Inner Experience*, p. 4.

38. On the koan in Zen Buddhism, see D. T. Suzuki, "The Koan Exercise," *Essays in Zen Buddhism: Second Series*, trans. Christmas

Humphreys (1933; Samuel Weiser, 1953), pp. 18–200. For Bataille's engagement with Buddhism, see in particular Bataille, *On Nietzsche*, pp. 81, 171–72.

39. On Bataille's meditational practices, see in particular Jean Bruno, "Les Techniques d'illumination chez Georges Bataille," *Critique* 195–96 (August–September 1963), pp. 706–20.

40. Bataille, *Inner Experience*, p. 52.

41. Bataille, *Inner Experience*, p. 120.

42. Jacques Lacan, *Encore: The Seminar of Jacques Lacan, Book XX*, trans. Bruce Fink (1972, 1975; W. W. Norton, 1998), p. 76.

43. Maurice Blanchot, *Faux pas*, trans. Charlotte Mandell (1943; Stanford University Press, 2001), p. 3.

44. Michel de Certeau has studied the historical forms of this discursive formation extensively. See Michel de Certeau, "Mystic Speech," *Heterologies: Discourse on the Other*, trans. Brian Massumi (University of Minnesota Press, 1986), 80–100, as well as *The Mystic Fable*, 2 vols., trans. Michael B. Smith (1982; University of Chicago Press, 1992–2015).

45. Bataille, *Guilty*, p. 14.

46. Bataille, *Inner Experience*, p. 95.

47. Bataille, *Guilty*, p. 9.

48. These poems are available in English in Bataille, *The Impossible*. The format and presentation of the original versions can be seen in Bataille, *L'Archangélique et autres poèmes*, Poésie (Gallimard, 2008), pp. 89–95.

49. Quoted in Jean-Yves Debreuille, "Poésie engagée et poésie dégagée," *Écrire sous l'Occupation: Du non-consentement à la Résistance*, ed. Bruno Curatolo and François Marcot (Presses universitaires de Rennes, 2011), p. 224.

50. Jean Lescure, *Poésie et liberté: Histoire de Messages, 1939–1946* (Éditions de L'IMEC, 1998), pp. 80–81.

51. A generation later, Guy Debord reasserted this idea forcefully in his *Panégyrique*: "The Gypsies rightly contend that one is never compelled to speak the truth except in one's own language; in that of the enemy, the lie must reign." See Debord, *Panégyrique, Tome Premier* (Gallimard, 1993), p. 20.

52. Lescure, *Poésie et liberté*, p. 84.

53. Bataille, *Erotism*, trans. Mary Dalwood (1957; City Lights Books, 1986), p. 258.

54. Lescure, *Poésie et liberté*, p. 177.

55. See Bataille, "Nietzsche's Laughter" (1942), *The Unfinished System of Nonknowledge*, ed. Stuart Kendall (University of Minnesota Press, 2001), pp. 18–25.

56. There were in fact two groups that Bataille organized under the name Socratic College that year. The other group included Pierre Prévost, Xavier de Lignac, Romain Petitot, Georges Pelorson, Louis Ollivier, and others, most of whom knew one another from their participation in the journal *Jeune France*, a journal to which Bataille did not contribute. Blanchot participated in both groups. For additional context, see Kendall, *Georges Bataille*, p. 165. See also, Bataille, "Socratic College" (1942), *The Unfinished System of Nonknowledge*, pp. 5–17.

57. See Lescure, *Poésie et liberté*, p. 181.

58. On Éditions de Minuit, see Anne Simonin, *Les Éditions de Minuit: 1942–1955, le devoir d'insoumission* (Éditions de L'IMEC, 1994).

59. Lescure, *Poésie et liberté*, p. 181.

60. Bataille, *On Nietzsche*, p. 10.

61. Bataille, *On Nietzsche*, p. 10.

62. Bataille, *Inner Experience*, p. 13.

63. Blanchot, *Faux pas*, p. 130.

64. Bataille, *Inner Experience*, pp. 135–36.

65. Bataille, *Inner Experience*, p. 135.

66. Bataille, *Guilty*, p. 93.

67. Bataille, "La Volonté de l'impossible" (1945), *Oeuvres complètes*, vol. 11 (Gallimard, 1988), p. 21.

68. Bataille, *Louis XXX*, trans. Stuart Kendall (Equus, 2013), p. 47.

69. Bataille, "La Volonté de l'impossible," p. 20.

70. Bataille, "La Volonté de l'impossible," p. 20.

71. Bataille, *Guilty*, p. 91.

72. Bataille, "La Littérature est-elle utile?" (1944), *Oeuvres complètes*, vol. 11, p. 13.

73. Bataille, *Inner Experience*, p. 258.

74. Bataille, "From the Stone Age to Jacques Prévert" (1946), *The Absence of Myth*, trans. Michael Richardson (Verso, 1994), p. 140.

75. Bataille, "From the Stone Age to Jacques Prévert," p. 152.

76. See Bataille, *Choix de lettres*, pp. 247, 257.

77. Bataille, *Inner Experience*, p. 149.

78. Bataille, *Inner Experience*, p. 20.

79. Bataille, *Literature and Evil*, p. 38. Bataille's article was occasioned by Jean-Paul Sartre's introduction to Charles Baudelaire, *Écrits intimes* (Point du jour, 1946); later released as a book, Sartre, *Baudelaire* (Gallimard, 1946); see Sartre, *Baudelaire*, trans. Martin Turnell (1946; New Directions, 1950).

80. Bataille, "Etre Oreste," *Romans et récits*, p. 594.

81. Bataille, *Inner Experience*, p. 55.

82. Bataille, *Inner Experience*, p. 135.

The Poetry of
Georges Bataille

Acéphale

Acéphale

O OBJECT
that you are empty
of me

O OBJECT
will you be empty
of yourself

Are you
the immensely empty ghost
of calm imaginations

The ghost decrees
with a distorted voice

WOE TO THOSE
WHO HEAR VOICES

Poems from *Inner Experience*

I don't want more, I moan
I can't suffer more
my prison.
I say this
bitterly:
Words that suffocate me,
leave me,
release me,
I am thirsty
for something else.
I want death
don't admit
this reign of words,
enchaining
without dread
such that dread
should be desirable;
it's nothing,
this self that I am,
if not
cowardly acceptance
of what is.
I hate
this instrumental life,
I seek a crack,
my crack,
to be shattered.
I love the rain
lightning
mud
a vast expanse of water

the depths of the earth
but not me.
In the depths of the earth,
O my tomb,
deliver me from myself,
I no longer want to be.

Ghost in tears
O dead God
hollow eye
damp mustache
single tooth
O dead God
O dead God
Me
I hounded you
with hatred
unfathomable
and I would die of hatred
as a cloud
is undone.

Manibus date lilia plenis *

Gloria in excelsis mihi   *

At the height of the heavens
the angels, I hear their voices, glorify me.
I am, under the sun, an errant ant,
small and black, a rolling stone
reaches me,
crushes me,
dead,
in the sky
the sun rages
it blinds,
I cry out:
"it will not dare"
it dares.

Who am I
not "me" no no
but the desert the night the immensity
that I am
what are
desert immensity night beast
quick nothingness without return
and without having known anything
Death
answer
sponge streaming with solar
dreams
sink into me
that I no longer know anything
but these tears.

Star
I am the star
O death
thunderous star
mad bell of my death

Poems
not courageous
but gentleness
ear of delight
a lamb's voice howls
beyond goes beyond
torch   extinguished.

God

With eager hands
I die you die
where is he
where am I
without laughter
I am dead
dead and dead
in the ink night
arrow shot
at   him.

Pain and Four Poems

Pain

Pain
pain
pain
O pain
O pain
O my pitch tears
my saffron cock

O pull my pants down
piss myself

Mademoiselle My Heart

Mademoiselle my heart
stripped naked in lace
perfumed mouth
piss running down her legs

The disguised odor of the crack
open to the wind of the sky

a cloud
in the head
reflects itself reversed
a marvelous star
falls
heart crying like a mouth

the heart fails
a lily is burning
the sun opens the throat.

Piss

Magpie eater of stars
fatigue eater of earth
exhaustion of everything

rapacious sky
cursed sky
partisan of the hospital

a raven on stilts
enters the eye   *

heart in ruby flames
piss on my naked thigh
smooth wet ass
I get hard and I cry

black wing of the tomb
politeness of the crypt.   *

The Roman Way

The Roman way
a veal heart
pointed beard
and the pink gland.

Laughter

Laugh and laugh
at the sun
at nettles
pebbles
ducks

at the rain
at the Pope's piss
at mama
at a coffin full of shit.

Poem from *The Little One*

Absence of Remorse

I have shit in my eyes
I have shit in my heart
God flows away
laughs
radiant
intoxicates the sky
the sky sings at the top of its lungs the sky sings
the thunder sings
solar lightning sings
dry eyes
broken silence of shit in the heart

*If a joyous gland engendered the universe, it would make
it as it is: one would have to, in the transparency of the sky,
of blood, of cries, of stink.*
God is not a priest but a gland: papa is a gland.

My crack is a friend
in the eyes of fine wine
and my crime is a friend
to brandied lips

I shake myself from reason
wipe myself from the apple

Poems from *Guilty*

Too much daylight too much joy too much sky   *
the earth too vast a fast horse
I hear the waters I cry for the day   *

The earth turns in my eyes
the stones roll in my bones
anemone and glowworm
bring me to a faint

In a shroud of roses
an incandescent tear
announces the day.   *

Absence of thunder
eternal expanse of crying waters
and me a smiling fly
and me a severed hand
I drenched my sheets
and I was the past
blind dead star   *

Yellow dog
there
horror
screaming like an egg
and vomiting my heart
absent a hand
I'm screaming

I scream at the sky that
it's not me who is screaming
in this lacerating thunderstorm
it's not me who is dying
it's the starry sky
the starry sky screams
the starry sky cries
I fall asleep
and the world is forgotten

Bury me in the sun
bury my loves
bury my wife
naked in the sun
bury my kisses
and my white drool.   *

Archangelic

The Tomb   *

I

Criminal immensity
vase cracked by immensity
limitless ruin   *

immensity overwhelms me gently
I am limp
the universe is guilty

winged madness my madness
lacerates the immensity
and the immensity lacerates me   *

I am alone
some blind men will read these lines   *
in interminable tunnels

I fall into the immensity
that falls into itself
it is blacker than my death

the sun is black   *
the beauty of a being is the depth of cellars a scream   *
of definitive night   *

the night's desire   *
loves in the light
the shiver in which it is frozen   *

38

I lie
and the universe nails itself
to my demented lies   *

the immensity   *
and I
denounce our lies each of the other   *

truth dies
and I scream
that truth lies

my sugared head
that exhausts fever
is the suicide of truth

Nonlove is truth
and everything lies in the absence of love
nothing exists that doesn't lie   *

Compared to nonlove
love is cowardly
and doesn't love

Love is a parody of nonlove   *
truth a parody of lies
the universe a gay suicide

In nonlove
the immensity falls into itself
not knowing what to do   *

Everything is peaceful for others   *
worlds turn majestically
in their monotonous calm

The universe is in me just as it is in itself
nothing separates us any longer
I throw myself into myself at it   *

In the infinite calm
where laws enchain
it slips toward the impossible immensely   *

Horror   *
of a world turning round   *
the object of desire is further away

The glory of man is
so great that it should be   *
from wanting an other

I exist
the world is with me
pushed outside the possible   *

I am only laughter
and the puerile night
wherein immensity falls   *

41

I am the dead man
the blind man
the shadow without air

Like rivers in the sea
in me noise and light
lose themselves without end

I am the father
and the tomb
of the sky

Excess of gloom   *
is the burst of a star
the cold of the tomb is a die

Death will throw the dice   *
and the depth of the sky jubilate
from the night that falls in me.   *

II

Time oppresses me I fall
and slide to my knees
my hands explore the night

Good-bye streams of light   *
only darkness, dregs, blood
remain for me

I await the tolling bell   *
when, crying out
I will enter into darkness.

III

A long naked foot on my mouth $*$
a long naked foot against my heart
you are my thirst my fever

Foot of whiskey
foot of wine
foot crazed to bring me down

O my whip my pain
high heel kicking me to the ground $*$
I cry out not to die

O thirst
unquenchable thirst
desert without end $*$

Sudden gust of death wherein I scream
blind on my knees
and empty sockets

Corridor wherein I laugh from a senseless night
corridor wherein I laugh in the slamming of doors
wherein I adore an arrow

And burst into sobs
the clarion call of death
roars in my ear.   *

IV

Beyond my death
one day
the earth turns in the sky

I am dead
and the shadows
alternate endlessly with the day   *

the universe is closed to me
I remain blind within it
wedded to nothingness

Nothingness is only my self
the universe is only my tomb
the sun is only death   *

My eyes are blind lightning
my heart is the sky
in which the storm breaks

In me
at the bottom of an abyss
the immense universe is dead

I am the fever
the desire
I am the thirst

The joy that pulls back the dress
and the wine that creates laughter
from no longer having a dress   *

In a shot of gin   *
a night of celebration
stars falling from the sky

I swallow the lightning in gulps
I'm going to laugh to bursting
lightning in my heart.

The Dawn

Spit blood
is the dew
the saber from which I was dying

From the edge of the pit
watching the starry sky
take on the transparence of tears.

I find you in the star
I find you in death
you are the frost in my mouth
you have the stench of a dead woman

Your breasts open like a coffin
and laugh at me from beyond
your long delirious thighs
your stomach is bare like a death rattle

You are beautiful like fear
you are mad like a dead woman.   *

The unhappiness is unnameable
the heart is a grimace

Floating around in milk
death the madwoman's laughter

A star raises itself
you are I am the void
a star raises itself
painful like the heart

Shimmering like a tear
you hiss it's death
the star fills the sky
painful as a tear   *

I know that you don't love
but the star that raises itself
cutting like death
exhausts and contorts the heart.*

I am cursed that's my mother   *
this night is long
my long night without tears   *

Night greedy for love
O broken heart of stone
the hell of my mouth of ash   *

You are the death of tears   *
be cursed
my cursed heart my sick eyes seek you

You are the void and the ash
headless bird, wings beating the night   *
the universe is made of your slight hope

The universe is your sick heart and mine
scraping the edge of death
at the cemetery of hope

My pain is the joy   *
and the ash the fire.

Tooth of hate
you are cursed
and the cursed will pay

You will pay your share of hate
you will bite the horrible sun   *
and the cursed bites the sky

With me you will tear
your fear-loving heart
your being strangled by boredom   *

You are the friend of the sun
there is no rest for you
your fatigue is my madness.

Manure mind   *
I burst I hate the sky
who am I to spit clouds
it's bitter being immense   *
my eyes are fat pigs
my heart is of black ink
my sex is a dead sun

The stars fall in a bottomless pit   *
I cry and my tongue slurs
it matters little that the immensity should be round
and move in a basket all its own
I love the death I invite
into the butcher shop of our Holy Father.

Black death you are my bread
I eat you at heart
terror is my sweetness
madness is in my hand.

Knot the rope of the hanged man
with the teeth of a dead horse   *

Gentleness of water
rage of wind

Burst of laughter from the star
morning of beautiful sunlight   *

It is nothing that I dream
it is nothing that I scream

Further than tears death
higher than the depths of the sky

In the space of your breasts.   *

Limpid from head to toe
fragile as the dawn
the wind has shattered the heart   *

For the duration of anguish
the black night is a church
wherein one slaughters a pig   *

Trembling from head to toe
fragile as death
agony my great sister

You are colder than the earth.   *

You meet happiness
watching it die

Your sleep and your absence
accompany it in the tomb.   *

You are the beating of the heart
that I hear beneath my skin
and in my suspended breath.   *

My sobs on your knees
I will shake the night

Shadow of wings across a field
my lost child's heart.

My laughing sister you are death
my failing heart you are death
in my arms you are death

We've been drinking you are death
like the wind you are death
like lightning death

Death laughs death is joy.   *

Only you are my life
of lost sobs
separating me from death
I see you through tears
and I divine my death

If I don't love death
pain
and desire for you
will kill me

Your absence
your distress
nauseates me
time for me to love death
time for death to bite my hands.

To love is to agonize   *
To love is to love to die
apes stink when dying   *

Enough, I want my death
I am too weak for this
enough, I am tired

Enough, I love you like a fool
I laugh at myself the ass of ink
braying at the stars in the sky   *

Naked you burst into laughter
gigantic under the canopy
in the end I beg to no longer exist

I want to die of you
I would like to annihilate myself
in your sick whims.

The Void

Flames surrounded us
the abyss opens under our steps
a silence of milk of frozen marrow
enveloped us with a halo

You are the transfigured one
my fate has broken your teeth
your heart is a hiccup
your fingernails found the void

You speak like laughter
the winds dress your hair
anguish grips your heart
precipitating your mockery

Your hands behind my head   *
knowing only death
your laughing kisses only open
at my hellish poverty

Under the sordid canopy
where the bats hang   *
your marvelous nudity
is but a lie without tears

My scream calls you in the desert
where you don't want to go
my scream calls you in the desert
where your dreams will be fulfilled

Your mouth sealed to my mouth
and your tongue in my teeth
the immense death will welcome you
the immense night will fall

Thus I will have made the void
in your abandoned head
your absence will be naked
like a leg without end

Waiting for the disaster   *
wherein the light will be extinguished
I will be gentle in your heart
like the chill of death.

Eleven Poems Withdrawn from *Archangelic*

My madness and my fear
have big dead eyes
the fixity of fever

Gazing in these eyes
is the nothingness of the universe
my eyes are blind skies

In my impenetrable night
is the impossible crying
everything collapsing   *

Almanac of ink soap
immortality of hairy poet
poetry cemetery of obesity

Good-bye saucy white meat
gentle death clothed in naked women

Good-bye false sleep

Infinite itching of ants arrest   *
group of papers mustache in dust
cartloads of fever

Colonnade of mad rain
clatter of soiled shrouds
funereal immodesty of human bones

There a madwoman heaps boxes of maybe
a policeman in shirtsleeves on top of a roof
signals something wrong the Demon   *

I lose you in the wind
I count you among the dead
a necessary rope
between wind and heart

I have nothing to do with this world
if not to burn
I love you in dying

Your absence of repose
a mad wind whistles in your head
you are sick to have laughed
you fled me for a bitter void
that tore your heart   *

Tear me up if you want to
my eyes find you in the night
burning with fever.   *

I'm cold at heart I tremble
from the depths of suffering I call you
with an inhuman cry
as if I gave birth

You strangle me like death
I know this miserably
I find you only in agony
you are beautiful like death

All words strangle me

Star pierce the sky
cry like death
strangle

I don't want life
strangling me is a kindness
the star that rises
is cold like a dead woman

Excite me, eyes
I love the night
my heart is black

Push me into the night
everything is false
I suffer

The world feels death
birds fly eyes slashed open
you are somber as a black sky

The festival will begin
in filth and fear

The stars will fall
when death approaches.

You are the horror of the night
I love you like a death rattle
you are weak like death

I love you like delirium
you know that my head dies
you are the immensity the fear

You are beautiful like slaughter
enormous heart I suffocate
your stomach is naked as the night.   *

You bring me straight to the end
the agony has begun
I have nothing more to tell you
I speak from the grave
and the dead are silent.

Two Poems from the
Manuscripts for *Archangelic*

I put my cock . . .   *

I put my cock against your cheek
the end brushes your ear
lick my balls slowly
your tongue is soft as water

Your tongue is raw as a butcheress
red as a leg of lamb
its tip is a cuckoo crying
my cock sobs with saliva

Your behind is my goddess
it opens like your mouth
I adore it like the sky
I venerate it like a fire

I drink in your laceration   *
I spread your naked legs
I open them like a book
wherein I read that which kills me.

O skull . . .

O skull anus of the empty night
this that dies the night the breath
the wind carries absence to obscurity

Deserted a sky falsifies being
empty voice heavy tongue of coffins
being strikes being
the head steals being
the sickness of being vomits a black sun of spit.

Blouse pulled up across
water flowered with hairs
when dirty happiness licks her lettuce
the sick heart
from the rain to the vacillating light of the spittle
    she laughs happily.

Poems from *On Nietzsche*

I imagine: an object of attraction,   *
the flame
shining and light
consuming itself in itself
annihilating itself
and in this way revealing emptiness,
the identity of the attraction,
of that which intoxicates
and of the void;

I imagine
emptiness
identical to the flame,
the suppression of the object
revealing the flame
that intoxicates
and illuminates.

And I cry out   *
unhinged
what is
hopeless

in my heart is hidden
a dead mouse   *

the mouse dies
hunted down

and in my hand the world is dead
the old candle blown out
before I go to bed

sickness the death of the world
I am the sickness
I am the death of the world.   *

Silence in my heart
at the violent gust of wind
my temples throbbing with death
and a black star falls
in my erect skeleton

black
silence I invade the sky   *
black my mouth is an arm
black
writing on a wall in flames
black
the empty wind of the tomb
whistles in my head.

The mad silence of a step
the silence of a hiccup
where is the earth where the sky

And the distraught sky
I go mad

I deceive the world and I die
I forget and I bury it
in the tomb of my bones.

O my absent
death's-head eyes.   *

Hope   *
O my rocking horse
in the darkness a giant
I am this giant
on a rocking horse.

Starry sky
my sister
cursed men
star you are death
the light of a great cold

solitude of lightning
absence of humanity at last
I empty myself of memories
a desert sun
effaces my name

star I see
its silence ice
it cries out like a wolf
on my back I fall to the ground
it kills me I guess.   *

O the dice thrown
from the depths of the tomb
in the fingers of the delicate night

dice from birds of sunlight
leaps from the drunk lark
me like an arrow
out of the night

O transparency of bones
my heart drunk with sunlight
is the shaft of the night.   *

Disparate Poems

Circumstantial Poem

To the point of exhaustion in the eyes
to the point of tears from the mud
to the point of hands swollen with pus
leads the road of defiance

Long death rattles from the grave
wherein a dead woman whistled without air
and from the absence of hope
the star of nudity was born.

(November 1943)

Poem Written without Being Entirely Awake   *

          *

I gave to Limbour a rendezvous
on the Champs-Elysées
to speak of heaven

I said
heaven is a cat

A third said
heaven is two cats

Another said
heaven is a tongue
thicker than a mob.

Sonnet *

*

I dreamed of touching the sadness of the world *
on the disenchanted bank of a strange marsh
I dreamt of a heavy sea in which I rediscovered
the lost road of your deep mouth

I felt in my hands a filthy animal *
escaped in the night from a frightful forest
and I saw that it was the evil from which you died *
that I call while laughing the sadness of the world

A mad light a burst of thunder
a liberating laugh your long nudity
an immense splendor illuminated me in the end *

And I live your pain as a charity
radiating in the night the long clear form
and the cry of the tomb of your infinity *

Two Poems Expressing Lost Love

Dying I would like to hold
the object you will give me
to grip in my frozen hand
then dirty it with my lips
with the spit of agony.

Dressed in my blood sweat
disheveled phantom of an old woman
the wind will freeze your teeth
so I will kiss them
you will be dead.

Erotic Poem

The depth of a night
buries in its dust
the great star Butchery
....
the MILK of the sky.

Poems from
The Tomb of Louis XXX

Dregs
the exhaustion of an odious heart
acrid
the gentle intimacy of vice

The SKY inverted in your eyes.

Tomb of the wind   *
Tomb of the river

My death falsifies my voice
which only reaches

Aching teeth

Little flower
you know little ear   *
the extent to which
I'm afraid of shit.

At night
look at the sky
with the crack behind.   *

The wound is fresh
disfiguring
the red streams
the cut hardens

there is no longer any eye
it's me.

Eliminated Poems and
Other Unpublished Poems

The Houses

Ten hundred houses fall
one hundred then one thousand dead
at the window of nudity   *

An empty pain
string of shadows
this night extends its suffocation

The eyes of these dead
exhaust the heart
blind mute head
dementia without being.

Even the hole of the stars
even the ink night
even the extinguished eye
even a great silence
even the haunted chateau of my memories
even a madwoman's scream
even anguish even the tomb

Even the dawn of my death.

The Ossuary

The force of life and the misfortune of the cold
the hard stupidity of man
knowing the law of his knife
head greedy for ecstasy

An icy heart a steaming soup
a foot dirty with blood
mustache of tears
a death rattle.   *

The Wall

An axe
give me an axe
since I'm afraid
of my shadow on the wall
boredom
empty feeling
fatigue.

The Parvis

Nightcap
chamber pot
red stocking dentures

gold miter
a frozen sky
eats the softness of the perched cat.

Endless face
of God
this gentleman
and his lady
etc.
I die of this
and you.   *

The Chateau

My little pains
tear me to pieces at night
rending me to ruin
at the summit of a bald rock

A crumbling wall
climbing the black sky
raising the dead stone
of a dreadful tower.

Frost

My lover death
star of living lime
ice heart water heart
heart hairy with frost
star of ash
silence without lips.   *

The Window   *

Little bird
thousand colors
a death empties the sky

A flat raven   *
dead eyes
wind tears the sky

Whispers
of a dead woman
madness opens the sky.

Mass of earth in the sky
silent sign of nothingness
dull yellow grassy mountain
fall of being in the night

I hide myself in your shadows
and I eat your sun
my skeleton revealed
in the light of day

A feeling of terror
gently grips the throat
it slowly chills the heart.

The Ground

I love the ash the burned stone
a head of hard stone
and the insistence of my life

Purplish hands
laughter in the cold
and the red knife of the teeth.   *

The Seminary

Thirty black souls
frozen jaws
thirty black asses   *
mangy jaws

A dead star
sings a psalm miserere
a dead mouth
spits a soul miserere

A sky of ass
sneezes a cry of fear
wherein my soul
spit its cares.

Bird's laughter filthy with blood
crash of ice from teeth
filth scream vomiting
head hung in horror.

Earth turn turn earth
a wooden whore turning a trick   *
red sun black sun
roses white roses roses

roses from tombs
turning roses
whores of tombs
turning tombs.

Cracked skull   *
burning city

Sooty sky
hairy woman

Flayed rabbit
dripping nose.

The Mask

Death masked in thick paper
flee the excess of this silence
amuse the stench.

The Church

Kiss of winter
O my dying sister
glimmer of wolf's hungry snap
stone of frost even the naked heart

Ah indifferent spit
ah sky insulting to every heart
ah cold more empty than death.

The wolf sighs . . .

The wolf sighs tenderly   *
sleep beautiful damsel
the wolf cried like a child
never will you know my pain
the wolf cried like a child

Beauty laughed at her lover
wind wailed in a great oak   *
the wolf died crying blood
his bones drying on the plain
the wolf died crying blood.

Lost in the thunderheads   *
without eyes my head is laughing
I am not the sun
heads fall in tombs

The fat superfluous head
the wall swells the soft
currant bush in the wind
night and day empty it

Value in relation to what?   *
Indifferent to myself
(I see)
what encircles me
calm, empty expanse
that is nothing
the absence of limits
escapes me in every way

The immensity annihilates itself
at the same time that it annihilates me

(I am no longer anything)
but a slippage into this empty expanse

Everything slips away
slowly
(I am bound by the weight of the earth
but) the earth slips away
in a movement in which each thing is separated
and floats
carried by the immense movement
that is neither the fall nor the absence of the fall
but that opens infinitely
vertiginously
in all space

In the space of your heart   *
I fall it's emptiness
at the dawn of swallows
lacerating your immensity
will I laugh in this sky   *

I'm striped like an arrow
your absence blood flowed
beyond my strange laughter
you are in the pure wind
you are the day   *

Your happiness
irradiates the rooftops
it lacerates the naked   *
you are my arrow my sword
the thread the sunlight   *

You are the flame that dies   *
the transparency of cries
your laughter is the mad dawn
pure freedom
of naked breasts.   *

Whiteness veiled by damp vapors   *
or blue
leaving the untouchable horror naked   *

low or pure sky
dead and without beginning or end   *
hair of hissing snakes on my head

burst of my white eyes   *
when I've had too much to drink
when I fall down wanting to vomit

viper
that I hate
from which I turn my eyes away

innocent sky, luminous, laughable
snake with knotted head
you are a joke   *

II

my hands strangled the sky
they laughed
and already fell asleep

in folds of light
hiding my sickness
my tears venom [of?] my shame   *

vermin of coal smoke
smothering the night expecting a storm
a child's anguish

pitched from blood from venom
my feverish hands   *
content with a good turn   *

Undifferentiated Being Is Nothing

I

Cap
of felt   *
of death
frost
sister
of a sob
joyful

the whiteness
of the sea
and the pallor of the light
will disrobe the bones of the dead   *

the absence
of the dead
smiles.

II

The body
of delight
is the heart
of this delirium.   *

III

The laws of taste
lay siege to
the tower of luxury.

IV

The alcohol
of poetry
is silence
defunct.

*

V

I puked   *
through the nose
spider sky
my shrunken temples
complete the thinning
I am dead   *
and the lilies
evaporate distilled water   *

Words fail

And I fail in the end.   *

VI

The words of the poem, their indiscipline, their number, their insignificance, restrain the heart in an impalpable instant, a slow kiss, dwelling on the mouth of a dead woman; the words suspend the breath that is no longer.

The transparency of the beloved, her miraculous indifference, is lost, lost in the numberless crystals of light: never to think again.

VII

The lightning kills
rolls eyes back
joy
effaces
joy

Effaced
window of death
frozen
O glass
glittering
from a burst that shatters
in the shadows themselves

I am
that which is not
I open
the conflicted teeth
of the dead
and the grating of the light
that intoxicates me
from the grip
that suffocates itself
with water
that cries
from the dead air
and of the soul of oblivion

But nothing
I see
nothing
I no longer laugh
since through the force of laughter
I am revealed.

Erotic Poems

Insignificance   *

I dull
the needle
of my heart
I cry
a word
that I lost
I open
the edge
of a tear
where the dead
dawn
silences itself.

Before Dawn

I efface
the step
I efface
the word
the space
and the breath
failing.

The Earth   *

The dead
seized the quick

and the bird closes the procession.

The Wash ⁣   *

The moon
is the soap
of the shrill pipe
my voice.

I open the legs   *
to the tongue of beef
of fur

A long penis spit
into the church of my heart.

My little hole is the altar
whose cloth is the shithouse.

The dead sun lit up the hairy shadow
of a trail of bitter sperm
the head of your tongue to the eyes of blood.

Swollen like a penis my tongue
in your throat of pink love.

My vulva is my butchery
red blood washed in sperm
sperm swims in blood.   *

In my mauve stockings apple perfume
pantheon of the majestic dick
a bitch's ass open
to the holiness of the street.

Hairy love of my leg
pantheon of sperm   *

I sleep
mouth open in waiting
for a penis to strangle me
from a dull spurt to a sticky one.   *

The ecstasy that screws me is the marble
of the virgin stained with blood.

Deliver me to cocks
I put on
my dress to tear open your soul.   *

The bird
of the wood
and solitude
of the forest.

*

Lightning

The cannon resounds in the body
and the lightning in the bronze eye
has the nudity of filth.

Solitude

Thumb in the cunt
sacred vase on the naked breasts
my ass soils the cloth of the altar
my mouth implores O Christ
the charity of your thorn.

Sleepless Night

To strangle oneself
to stunt a voice
to swallow the dying tongue
to abolish the noise
to go to sleep
to shave
to laugh at angels.

Black Night

You will mock your neighbors as yourself

Drag love from the goose
from the spleen of great men

Oblivion is the friendship of the slaughtered

Reverence speaks
I leave.

Death Knell

In my voluptuous bell
death's bronze dances
the clapper of a prick sounds
a long libidinous swing

*

The Bald

The hole of your prick is the laughter
of which your testicles are the dawn.

Coryphea   *

Coryphea

Misfortune! Blood flows from my breasts, my gullet opens to death at the sound of wretched gurgling . . . I give my life to cunning smiles of pleasure: the intoxicating smell of money. Let one final embrace offer your loins a dress sticky with death.

Five Poems from 1957

My Song

I fill the sky with my presence
My cry is not that
of a large bird
that pierces the dawn
my song is not that
of the cicadas filling the summer nights
my lament is not that of the ones
agonizing in the void
that follows a bombardment
it lacerates
I don't die I am nothing
do I know the nature of this cry
it opens the clouds
I don't laugh
I never cry
I howl   *
I open the sky
the way you open the throat
of the dying
I am calm
like a bull
bellowing in the rain
I am not a man
I bellow
I am more foolish than lightning
bursting with laughter
I want to make so much noise
that no one will ever hear anything again

The Marseillaise of Love

Two naked lovers sing the Marseillaise
two bloody kisses chew their hearts
horses charge
horsemen dead
village abandoned
the child cries
in the interminable night

The Brown Waltz

The Chameleon
takes the accordion
guitar
its string broken
the bride full of liqueur
and the waltz dies
to the tune of *Libera nos*   *

It's the New Dance

When mules
die of cholera
the mule's sob
is a widow's sob
and the widow
dreams of her loves
crying crying
until the end of the world
dreaming dreaming
of our failed loves
this is not the time to brag
today
but tomorrow
all the asses of the world
dance the cholera

[The Sidewalk of Danaides]   *

My whore
my heart
I love you the way one shits
Soak your ass in the storm
surrounded by lightning
The lightning kisses you
a madman wails in the night
getting hard like a stag
O death I am this stag
that devours dogs
Death ejaculates in blood

Notes

The manuscripts for Bataille's poetry are more heavily worked than many of his other writings. Frequently, successive drafts evidence wider variance than is typical of Bataille: words are changed, line breaks are shifted, stanzas and whole poems are reworked, reused in new combinations, or abandoned altogether. In some cases, drafts for poems were often reserved and reworked over two or more years. Sometimes the differences between poems and other types of writing, particularly meditations and notes, is unclear. This is doubly challenging in works that explicitly undermine the notion of poetic language, as these do.

As discussed in the introduction, Bataille wrote poetry only occasionally during his career as a writer. Those occasions, however, resulted in the production of a great deal of poetry during more or less concentrated periods of time, which Bataille then edited, rewrote, or otherwise reworked into final form. Final form for Bataille and in regard to his poetry also often meant sequential form. Most of Bataille's poetry falls into more or less tightly organized groups of poems, occasionally in a loosely narrative order.

Bataille published only fifty-nine poems—slightly less than half of the present volume—during his lifetime. The majority of those poems appeared in one large thematically linked volume, Archangelic *(1944); the others often appeared as part of his other works, including his major works* Inner Experience *(1943),* Guilty *(1944), and* On Nietzsche *(1945). Bataille also published a few poems in journals and reviews prior to the appearance of those poems in books. On a few occasions Bataille included poems in more than one work, as when he used a poem from* Archangelic *as an epigraph to* Guilty. *Of the poems Bataille published, some appeared in volumes intended for wide circulation, while others were printed in small press editions intended only for private circulation.*

The present volume, however, includes both poems that Bataille published and poems that he did not. Of the poems Bataille did not publish, some were prepared for publication but ultimately abandoned prior to publication, occasionally for unknown or obscure reasons. Many other poems were found among his manuscripts in draft state. In some cases, there are multiple drafts and variants even of unpublished poems.

Since more than half of Bataille's poetry was unpublished at the time of his death, it is important to distinguish, in the structure of a volume collecting all of Bataille's poetry, those pieces that he published from those pieces that he did not, as well as to group together poems that were clearly written during distinct periods or that were associated with one another by Bataille as he organized his manuscripts. The sections of this volume are organized in order to facilitate this approach to the work. They are presented in roughly chronological order, with the caveat that many of these poems and groups of poems were written or edited alongside one another, in most cases over a period of just a few years, 1942 to 1945. The notes that follow provide information in regard to the first publication of the poems as well as variant readings from manuscripts, drafts, or early publications. As a rule, this volume presents the final versions of the works collected herein, even when that final version remains only a draft.

In French, Bataille's poetry can be found in volumes 3, 4, 5, and 6 of his Oeuvres complètes, *12 vols., ed. Thadée Klossowksi (Gallimard, 1970–88) as well as in a separate volume,* Archangélique et autres poèmes, *ed. Bernard Noël, collection Poésie (Gallimard, 2008). The Pléiade edition of Bataille's fiction includes some of his poetry as well:* Romans et récits, *ed. Jean-François Louette et al., Bibliothèque de la Pléiade (Gallimard, 2004). In the notes that follow, I have collated and adapted the relevant notes from each of these volumes, as well as providing additional contextual and intertextual annotation for anglophone readers and readers who may be unfamiliar with Bataille's other writings. As noted in the introduction, like all of his writing, Bataille's poetry is densely intertextual, shot through with references to figures, scenes, and ideas explored in his other works and the works of writers—most notably, Nietzsche, Angela of Foligno, and St. John of the Cross—who influenced him. Only on rare occasions have I annotated these references.*

I have previously published translations of a number of the poems included here. Some of those translations appeared in Inner Experience *(State University of New York Press, 2014),* Guilty *(State University of New York Press, 2011),* On Nietzsche *(State University of New York Press, 2015),* The Little One *and* The Tomb of Louis XXX *(see* Louis XXX *[Equus Press, 2013]), and* The Unfinished System of Nonknowledge *(University of Minnesota Press, 2001). I have nevertheless taken this opportunity to revisit these works with a fresh eye informed by my ongoing engagement with Bataille's work and the context created by this volume. Discrepancies between the translations of poems included in these works and the translations in the current volume should be understood in this light and with the caveat that every translation is itself an interpretation, and is therefore also provisional.*

Titles for works published or prepared for publication by Bataille are Bataille's own. All other titles originated with the Gallimard editors, Bernard Noël or Thadée Klossowski.

The Poetry of Georges Bataille

Acéphale

Undated. Unpublished. Maurice Blanchot shared this poem by Bataille with Bruno Roy as part of his contribution to G. L. M., *a volume published by Fata Morgana in 1982 in homage to Guy Levis Mano, who published, among many significant contributions to French letters, the first four issues of the journal* Acéphale *in 1936 and 1937. Bataille met Blanchot toward the end of 1940 or beginning of 1941. Our text appears in* L'Archangélique et autres poèmes, *collection Poésie (Gallimard, 2008), p. 145.*

Poems from *Inner Experience*

Published by Éditions Gallimard, 1943. Written late fall 1941 through summer 1942. Our text is Bataille, Oeuvres complètes, *vol. 5 (Gallimard, 1973), pp. 71–72, 121, 185–89. See Bataille,* Inner Experience *(State University of New York Press, 2014), pp. 61–62, 105, 159–65.*

12   Manibus date lilia plenis. *(Gives lilies with full hands) Virgil, Aeneid bk. 6, ln. 883. Mourning the death of Marcellus, nephew of Augustus. This line is quoted by Dante upon leaving Virgil in* Purgatory *canto 30, ln. 21.*

13   Gloria in excelsis mihi. *(Glory to myself the highest) This is a play on "Gloria in excelsis Deo" (Glory to God the highest).*

Pain and Four Poems

Unpublished. These poems were found, along with two drafts for The Little One, *among manuscripts for* The Tomb of Louis XXX. *A title page found among them, though not necessarily for these poems, reads: "Erotic Poems, Paris and Panilleuse, October and November 1942." Panilleuse is a small village in Normandy near Mantes and Tilly where Bataille spent much of the fall of 1942. Our text is Bataille,* Oeuvres complètes, *vol. 4 (Gallimard, 1971), pp. 11–13.*

Piss

23   enters the eye. *A first draft reads:* enters the eye and crows.

23   crypt. Crypt *(caveau)* or head *(cerveau)? Illegible.*

Poem from *The Little One*

Published privately by Bataille under the pseudonym Louis Trente, with the help of publisher Georges Hugnet, in June 1943. The original text carried the false but personally significant date 1934. The manuscript for this poem appears in a notebook for Archangelic *dating from 1942 to 1943. Our text is Bataille,* Oeuvres complètes, *vol. 3 (Gallimard, 1971), p. 65. For my translation of the full text of* The Little One, *see Bataille,* Louis XXX *(Equus Press, 2013).*

Poems from *Guilty*

Published by Éditions Gallimard, 1944. Our text is Bataille, Oeuvres complètes, *vol. 5, pp. 314, 356–57. See Bataille,* Guilty *(State University of New York Press, 2011), pp. 64, 98–99.*

33 Too much daylight too much joy too much sky. *This poem is dated December 1, 1942.*

33 I cry for the day. *Manuscript:* I hear the day.

33 announces the day. *Manuscript:* My lightning my gentleness.

34 blind dead star. *Manuscript:*

> blind dead star
> and twelve rotten onions
> yellow dog
> *[. . .]*

34 and my white drool. *Manuscript continues, crossed out:*

> the sky went poopoo
> the sky went caca
> river birds
> and tide pools
> flowing with sleep
> coo *[cooing?]* with pleasure
> the beautiful throat cries
> and the long black hair
> laughing with kisses
> flies bees
> cows elephants
> trumpeting making love
> I am an elephant
> I am a cow I am a glass
> of white wine

Archangelic

Published by Éditions Messages, Paris, 1944. The book was printed in an edition of 113 copies, all hors commerce, on April 30, 1944. The first part, "The Tomb," had already appeared separately under the title "La Douleur" (Pain) in an anthology, Domaine Français *(Éditions Messages/Éditions*

Trois-Collines, 1943). Written primarily in Vézeley, between August and December 1943, with additional poems written between October 1943 and April 1944 (see below). Our text is Bataille, Oeuvres complètes, *vol. 3, pp. 71–96, 500–08.*

A manuscript note from October 16, 1943, outlines a project involving these poems and other works.

First page:

I would like to do a book in place of the one *[Archangelic?]* that is projected with:

> The Solar Anus *[written in 1927, published in 1931; see Bataille,* Visions of Excess: Selected Writings, 1927–1939, *ed. Allan Stoekl (University of Minnesota Press, 1985), pp. 5–9]*
> Dirty *[written in 1928, published in 1945; see Bataille,* Blue of Noon, *trans. Harry Mathews (Marion Boyars, 1986), pp. 11–20]*
> The countryside *[unidentified]*
> Absence *[unidentified]*
> Erotic poems *[see* Pain and Four Poems *elsewhere in this volume]*
> The tomb

Plus the following poems:

> Spit blood
> I find you in the star
> The unhappiness is unnamable
> A star raises itself
> I am cursed that's my mother
> Tooth of hate
> Manure mind
> Black death you are my bread
> Unhappiness has horses *[an early draft of "Knot the rope of the hanged man"]*

Nothing else
As title for the book: DEAE DIANAE

Second page:

DEAE DIANAE

The Solar Anus
Dirty
The countryside
Absence
The Blind Man *[unidentified]*
Erotic Poems

DIANUS and DIANE

1. The Tomb
2. continuation of poems (see preceding page)
3. Deae Dianae

Bataille's papers include four manuscripts for Archangelic *as well as the text of the initial printing in* Domaine Français, *a notebook containing these and other poems, and separate draft sheets.*

37 The Tomb. *Manuscript and* Domaine Français: Pain.

38 limitless ruin. *Manuscript 1:* limitless damage.

38 and the immensity lacerates me. *Manuscripts and* Domaine Français: *but the immensity lacerates me. The manuscripts also separate these first three stanzas from the rest of the opening poem, indicating that they constitute a distinct poem within the section.*

38 some blind men will read these lines. *Manuscript 1:* . . . my lines.

38 the sun is black. *Manuscripts do not separate these two stanzas. These two line endings are also variant:*

    . . . than death
    . . . night

This line recalls the phrase "Night is also a sun" from Nietzsche's Thus Spoke Zarathustra *that Bataille often quoted, including as an epigraph to* Inner Experience. *See* Nietzsche, The Portable Nietzsche, *trans. Walter Kaufmann (Viking, 1954), p. 435.*

38   the beauty of a being is the depth of cellars a scream.
       Manuscript 1: the beauty of an angel is the depth of cellars.
       Manuscript 2: the beauty of a girl is the depth of cellars a scream.
       Manuscripts 3, 4, and Domaine Français: the scream.

38   of definitive night.
       Manuscript 1: the glare of a moment in a night without return.
       Manuscript 2 and Domaine Français: definitive darkness.

38   the night's desire.
       Manuscript 1: the haste of the night.
       Manuscript 2: the fall of the night.

38   the shiver in which it is frozen. Domain Français: the shiver that freezes it.

39   to my demented lies.
       Manuscript 1: my execrable lies.
       Manuscript 2, 3, 4, and Domaine Français: . . . demented lies.

39   the immensity. *Manuscript 1:*

       I lie because it lies
       the immensity and me
       the one to the other, both lie

39   denounce our lies each of the other.
       Manuscripts 2, 3, 4, and Domaine Français: denounce the impudence of each other.

40   nothing exists that doesn't lie. *Manuscript 1:* there is nothing in this world that . . .

40   Love is a parody of nonlove.

Manuscript 1:

Love is a parody of nonlove
truth a parody of lies
the universe a comic suicide

Manuscript 2:

Love, parody of nonlove
truth a parody of lies
the universe a gay suicide

Domaine Français:

Love, parody of nonlove

*On the theme of "nonlove" see, Angela of Foligno, Complete Works, ed.
and trans. Paul Lachance, Classics of Western Spirituality (Paulist Press,
1993), pp. 202ff.*

40   not knowing what to do.
      Manuscript 1: the immensity does not know what to do with itself.
      Manuscript 3:

      Love is a parody of non-love
      the immensity falls into itself
      not knowing what to do

40   Everything is peaceful for others. *Manuscript 1:* Everything seems
      peaceful for others.

40   I throw myself into myself at it. *In manuscript 1, followed by
      these two lines:*

      If it is calm *[crossed out:* I cannot be*]*
      I drive it to conquer death

40   it slips toward the impossible immensely. *In manuscript 1, this
      stanza is crossed out:*

189

It is death
it touches the impossible immensely
slipping toward the impossible immensely.

41   Horror. *In manuscript 1, precèded by these two lines:*

Peaceful bliss is guilty
coming in peace feeds remorse

In manuscript 2 and Domaine Français, *this becomes:*

Calm pleasures are guilty
coming without cries
feeds remorse

41   of a world turning round. *Manuscript 1:* . . . on itself turning round.

41   so great that it should be. *Manuscript 1:* something so great . . .

41   pushed outside the possible. *Manuscript 1:* . . . beyond the possible.

41   wherein immensity falls. *Manuscript 1:*

Man is the night
wherein immensity sinks
[crossed out: he is*]*
alone and puerile

Manuscript 2 and Domaine Français*:*

And alone, little child
man is the night
wherein immensity sinks

Manuscript 3:

I am only laughter
only a childish night
wherein immensity sinks

43   Excess of gloom. *Manuscript 1:* the excess of cold night.

43   Death will throw the dice. *Manuscript 1:* The dice thrown by death.

43   from the night that falls in me. *Manuscript 1:* from the cold that endures in my heart. Domaine Français *and manuscript 1 end here with the date Vézelay, August 1943.*

44   Good-bye streams of light. *Manuscript 2:* . . . *[crossed out:* streams*]* torrents . . .

44   I await the tolling bell. *Manuscript 2:* . . . the horrible tolling . . . *Manuscript 3:* . . . *[crossed out:* horrible*]* frightful tolling . . . *Manuscript 4:* . . . horrible tolling . . .

45   A long naked foot on my mouth. *Manuscript 2:* . . . the mouth.

45   high heel kicking me to the ground. *Manuscript 2:* . . . *[crossed out:* me to the ground*]* overwhelming me.

45   desert without end. *These last three lines are crossed out in manuscript 2, which also ends here.*

46   roars in my ear. *The drafts include eight successive versions of these three stanzas, the first of which is dated Vézelay, September 9 through 13, 1943.*

1.

Great sister of my death sister with wind in her hair
sister with a honeyed red mouth
grand corridor wherein I cry
kneeling in the blood of my dead eyes

Grand corridor wherein I laugh at being blind
grand corridor wherein I laugh at the slamming of doors
where I adore a fury where I die

The force of the wind of laughter of the day throws me
    to the ground

strike me I would die naked in a current of air slapped
    in the face
sound the trumpet in my ear

I see
dead eyes see
I see death

2.

The sister of my life has hair of vipers
a great laugh of a honeyed red
sudden current of air
burst of wind of death in which I cry
blind on my knees
and empty sockets

Corridor in which I laugh at my senseless night
corridor in which I laugh at the slamming of doors
in which I adore this wind that bursts in which I tremble

Weigh me down laughter at wind and wine
strike me I want to die naked in a current of air slapped
    in the face
alcohol life and broad daylight virile slap of my death
Sound a great trumpet blast in my ear

The beautiful tone of the singer of death

The final stanza then redone:

Alcohol laughing virile whip of my joy
make the blast of the immortal clarion of death
resound in my ear

3.

Sister of my death with whistling hair
domineering laugh of your honeyed red tongue
sudden blast of wind of my death wherein I cry

blind kneeling
and empty sockets

Corridor in which I laugh at my senseless night
corridor in which I laugh at the slamming of doors
in which I adore this wind that bursts in which I cry

Weigh me down laughter at wind and wine
strike me I want to die naked in a current of air slapped
    in the face
alcohol laughing virile whip of my joy
make the call of the clarion of my death
resound in my ear

4.

The light of my death has hair of vipers
Happy laughter of a honeyed red tongue
In a depthless sky of joy

Sudden gust of my death in which I cry

5.

Sudden gust of death wherein I scream
on my knees blind
empty sockets

Corridor wherein I laugh from my senseless night
corridor wherein I laugh in the slamming of doors
wherein I adore your lightning

And I fall sobbing
throw me to the ground laughter at wind and wine
strike me I want to die naked in a current of air slapped
    in the face

Kill me alcohol laughter virile sister of my fever
and roar in my ear
the clarion call of my death

193

6.

Sudden gust of death wherein I scream
blind on my knees
and empty sockets

Corridor wherein I laugh from my senseless night
corridor wherein I laugh in the slamming of doors
wherein I adore your lightning

Throw me to the ground storm of laughter and wine
slap me I want to die naked in a current of air slapped
    in the face

Smiling alcohol my virile sister kill me
and make the clarion call of my death
roar in my ear

7.

Sudden gust of death wherein I scream
blind on my knees
and empty sockets

Corridor wherein I laugh from a senseless night
corridor wherein I laugh in the slamming of doors
wherein I adore your lightning

Throw me to the ground storm of laughter and wine
slap me I want to die naked in a current of air slapped
    in the face

8.

Sudden gust of death wherein I scream
blind on my knees
and empty sockets

Corridor wherein I laugh from a senseless night
corridor wherein I laugh in the slamming of doors
wherein I adore a flame

And burst into sobs
the clarion call of death
roars in my ear.

Manuscripts 3 and 4 are the same as above except for the final line, which reads: has roared in my ear.

47   alternate endlessly with the day. *Three successive drafts:*

1.

As in the shadow on a lighthouse immensely
by turning causes the brightness and obscurity to dance
after my final rattle the earth in the sky
will alternate the brightness of the day and darkness
    without respite

beyond me and more true than me
more true than ever head or heart attained
which slips away from me and gets rid of me
I only dedicate myself to this by letting myself go
dark truth of which I am the light
absence of rest about which workers speak

2.

Even as immensely in dark skies
a lighthouse
by turning causes brightness and obscurity to dance

When I will be dead in this depthless sky
this globe continuing its course
will alternate the brightness of the day and the darkness
    without respite

3.

Beyond myself
one day
the earth will roll in the immensity

I will be dead
and the darkness
will alternate with the day without end

48   the sun is only death. *Draft of this first stanza:*

Only in me does death
look at the universe
and suffocate me

I am nothingness
the sun is my tomb
my absence is being.

49   from no longer having a dress. *Draft of these first two stanzas:*

I am the fever the impatience
and the unquenched desire
I am the laughter the vertigo

I am love pulling back the dress
and the wine that causes laughter
at a dress pulled back

In manuscript 4, alongside the final version, one reads:

I am the fever the desire
I am the thirst
the vertigo

I am the joy pulling back the dress
the wine that causes *[crossed out:* tears*]* laughter
at being naked

50   In a shot of gin. *Bataille used this poem as an epigraph to* Guilty.
     In manuscript 3, the poem is dated September 13, 1943. In manuscript
     4, alongside the final version, one reads:

     The stars fall
     In a shot of gin
     A night of celebration

53   you are mad like a dead woman. *Drafts and manuscript 3:* you
     are mad like one departed.

54   death the madwoman's laughter. *Draft, after a line break, continues:*

     eyes turn mouth swallows
     comic gall of joy

55   painful as a tear. *Manuscript 3:*

     painful as a blade
     complete me pain
     inexhaustible night

55   exhausts and contorts the heart. *Manuscript 3:* consumes the day.

56   I am cursed that's my mother. *Notebook:*

     I am cursed that's my mother
     child of the black night
     night is greedy for tears

     Night is greedy for love
     my broken heart of stone
     the hell of my mouth is ash

56   my long night without tears. *Manuscript 3:*

     child of a pale night
     immense night . . .

56   the hell of my mouth of ash. *Manuscript 3:*

    broken heart of stone
    the hell of my mouth of ash

56   You are the death of tears. *Notebook and manuscript 3:* . . . of my tears

56   headless bird, wings beating the night. *Notebook:* headless buzzard . . .

56   My pain is the joy. *Notebook and manuscript 3:* Pain is . . .

57   you will bite the horrible sun. *Notebook:* . . . the big sun

57   your being strangled by boredom. *Notebook:* your sky strangled . . .

58   Manure mind. *In the notebook, this poem is dated Friday, October 15, 1943, 11 p.m.*

58   it's bitter being immense. *Notebook and manuscript 3:* it's horrible . . .

58   The stars fall in a bottomless pit. *Notebook and manuscript 3:*

    The stars fall in a bottomless coffin
    the tongue flows and I cry
    it matters little that the immensity
    is round and falls in a basket all its own

60   with the teeth of a dead horse. *Notebook and manuscript 3:*

    Unhappiness has horses
    with heavy shoes
    the cold freezes in the heart
    and mad legs
    knot the rope of the hanged man
    with the teeth of a dead horse
    the depth of horror is my joy

61   morning of beautiful sunlight. *Notebook and manuscript 3: . . .*
broad daylight

61   In the space of your breasts. *Notebook and manuscript 3:*

> Further than unhappiness tears death
> higher than the depths of the skies
> in the space of your voice.

In the notebook, after a line break, the following lines (which also appear separately in manuscript 3, and in the final version):

> You meet happiness
> watching it die
>
> Your sleep and your absence
> accompany it in the tomb.

62   the wind has shattered the heart. *Manuscript 3:*

> a cold wind has shattered the heart
>
> the duration of anguish
> silence is a church

62   wherein one slaughters a pig. *Notebook:*

> the darkness is a church
> wherein one slaughters pigs

62   You are colder than the earth. *In manuscript 3, this poem is dated October 28, 1943.*

63   accompany it in the tomb. *In the notebook and in manuscript 3, this poem is part of the poem "Gentleness of water," see page 61.*

64   and in my suspended breath. *In the notebook, this poem comes after the next one.*

199

66 Death laughs death is joy. *Manuscript 3:* death laughs the bird cracks naked woman.

68 To love is to agonize. *Preceded in manuscript 3 by these lines:*

> In the black obscurity
> my nose banged hard into
> the column of the canopy

68 apes stink when dying. *Manuscript 3:* apes *[crossed out:* stink*]* spit when dying.

68 braying at the stars in the sky. *Manuscript 3:* hee-haw at the stars . . .

70 Your hands behind my head. *Manuscript 3:* . . . the head.

70 where the bats hang. *In the notebook and manuscript 3:*

> On a sordid canopy
> the worthless monkey is snuggled

71 Waiting for the disaster. *Notebook:* In expectation of the disaster. *Manuscript 3:*

> In expectation of the disaster
> in which the lights will be extinguished

Eleven Poems Withdrawn from *Archangelic*

Unpublished. Manuscript dated October 1943 to April 1944, in Vézeley and Paris. Our text is Bataille, Oeuvres complètes, *vol. 4, pp. 16–19.*

75 everything collapsing. *At the end of the poem, in the margin, we find a line that might be a possible title:* what I want.

77 Infinite itching of ants arrest. *This is preceded by these two crossed out stanzas:*

The place of my death is deserted
columns of rain
vaults of dawn and collapse

in the leggy grass milky flies
the mustache of a dead man has soft *[illegible:* soft *or*
mossy?] lips

77   signals something wrong the Demon. *Illegible line. The transcription may be inaccurate.*

79   that tore your heart. *Followed by this crossed out stanza (see "I put my cock . . . ," below, and* The Tomb of Louis XXX, *in Bataille,* Louis XXX, *p. 61).*

I spread your naked thighs
and your laceration offers itself
I divine the coming
of a deserted anxiety

79   burning with fever. *A first draft for this stanza:*

I don't want to be cured of you
heart in shreds I cry
tear me up I will die
transfixed by your big empty eyes.

84   your stomach is naked as the night. *Another version:* your stomach is mad like the dawn.

Two Poems from the Manuscripts for *Archangelic*

89   *I put my cock . . . Unpublished. Found among manuscripts for* Archangelic, *with other drafts dating from October 1943 to April 1944. The tone of the poem is, however, very different from that work, so the Gallimard editors present the poem separately. The Gallimard editors added the title of this poem. Our text is Bataille,* Oeuvres complètes, *vol. 4, p. 14.*

89　I drink in your laceration. *This final stanza appears as a separate poem entitled "The Book" in* The Tomb of Louis XXX *(see Bataille, Louis XXX, p. 61). Notes in that work indicate that it was to have been accompanied by a photograph of a woman's genitals, a vulva specifically.*

90　*O skull . . . Unpublished. Possibly two poems written on one page. Found with diverse manuscripts dating from before the war, linked by the Gallimard editors to* Archangelic *based on manuscript similarity. The Gallimard editors added the title of this poem. Our text is Bataille,* Oeuvres complètes, *vol. 4, p. 15.*

Poems from *On Nietzsche*

Published by Éditions Gallimard, 1945. Our text is Bataille, Oeuvres complètes, *vol. 6 (Gallimard, 1973), pp. 98–103. See Bataille,* On Nietzsche, *pp. 73, 87–92.*

93　I imagine: an object of attraction. *This first poem from* On Nietzsche *appears in a section of the manuscript that dates from March 1944. In the published text, the poem is preceded by this sentence:* "Expressing myself on a state designated by a shorthand name (*impalement*), I am writing these few lines in the form of a theme for meditation." On Nietzsche, *p. 73.*

94　And I cry out. *Bataille wrote these poems in a notebook on January 25, 1943, but did not include them, or the text immediately preceding them, in* Guilty, *which he was writing at the time. In the manuscript, they appear as one long poem with the title, written in English, "Time is out of joints." Bataille recopied the text for inclusion in* On Nietzsche *on April 12, 1944. See also Bataille,* Guilty, *p. 226n2.*

94　a dead mouse. *Manuscript 1943:*

> In my heart
> *[Crossed out:* is hidden*]* curled up together
> a white mouse

Manuscript of On Nietzsche*:*

> in my heart
> is hidden
> a dead mouse

94   I am the death of the world. *Manuscript 1943:*

> *[Crossed out:* I am*]* to be sickness
> *[Crossed out:* I am*]* to be the death to the world

95   silence I invade the sky. *Manuscript 1943:*

> black
> silence, I invade the sky
> black,
> my mouth is an arm
> *[. . .]*

Manuscript of On Nietzsche*:*

> silence I invade the sky
> black
> my mouth *[. . .]*

96   death's-head eyes. *Manuscript 1943:* O my absent eyes my eyes.

97   Hope. *Manuscript 1943:* January 26 *[1943]*.

98   it kills me I guess. *Manuscript 1943:*

> she kills me
> I guess

99   is the shaft of the night. *Manuscript 1943:*

> is the night
> the pole

Disparate Poems

Published as an appendix to the first edition of The Oresteia *(Editions de Quatre Vents, 1945). The titles are Bataille's. Our text is Bataille,* Oeuvres complètes, *vol. 3, pp. 543–44.*

104 Poem Written without Being Entirely Awake. *This poem was written in English.*

104 Limbour. *Georges Limbour (1900–70), a member of the surrealist group expelled in the second manifesto. He contributed to* Documents *and remained a friend of Bataille's thereafter. For Limbour's perspective on Bataille, see Georges Limbour, "Bibliothécaire à Carpentras" (1963),* Le Carnaval et les Civilisés *(L'Élocoquent, 1986), pp. 67–74.*

105 Sonnet. *A draft of this poem was found among manuscripts for* On Nietzsche *from March 1944. See Bataille,* On Nietzsche, *p. 266.*

105 I dreamt of touching the sadness of the world. *In the manuscript for* On Nietzsche, *this stanza is preceded by:*

> Your long nudity the animal forest
> the lost road of your deep mouth
> I dream of illuminating the sadness of the world

105 I felt in my hands a filthy animal. *In the manuscript for* On Nietzsche, *three crossed out versions of this line:*

> I held in my bed *[. . .]*
> I gripped in my arms *[. . .]*
> I held in my fingers *[. . .]*

105 and I saw that it was the evil from which you died. *At the end, two lines, thoroughly crossed out; possibly:*

> *[crossed out:* you laughed*]* while singing
> wandering among the flowers of the *[illegible]*
> *[word crossed out]* that I call *[. . .]*

105   an immense splendor illuminated me in the end. *In the manuscript for* On Nietzsche: *a splendor immense . . .*

105   and the cry of the tomb of your infinity. *In the manuscript for* On Nietzsche: *and the delirious cry of your infinity.*

107   Erotic Poem. *There are four manuscript versions of this final poem. The definitive version is set apart, the others are in different groups of poems that include, in each group, drafts for "Absence of Remorse," from* The Little One, *and the poems for* The Tomb of Louis XXX.

1. In the notebook (1942–43) for Archangelic, *four crossed out lines:*

> My Sunday is solitary
> my eye is solitary
> a saffron desert
> my hunger is solitary.

Followed by three illegible lines, then:

> Starry depth
> buried in your dust
> the butcher's long cock
> the milk that flows
>
> God you coo
> milk of the sky

2. Milk that flows *becomes:* milk of the sky.

*3. The two final lines—*God you coo / milk of the sky—*are suppressed.*

Poems from *The Tomb of Louis XXX*

Unpublished. The Tomb of Louis XXX *is another assemblage, like* The Oresteia, *combining poetry, prose, and, in this case, notes for images. As with* The Oresteia, *Bataille assembled* The Tomb of Louis XXX *from* manuscript materials written between 1942 and 1945. Bataille prepared the manuscript of The Tomb of Louis XXX for publication sometime prior to 1947, and there are three typed manuscript copies, one copy bearing annotations from a printer, though no copies of a printed version of the work have been found. The manuscript folder for the work also contains other groups of poems, including the poems gathered herein under the collective title Pain and Four Poems, as well as the poem from The Little One. For my translation of the complete text of The Tomb of Louis XXX, see Bataille, Louis XXX. Our text for these poems is Bataille, Oeuvres complètes, vol. 4, pp. 153–54.

L'Archangélique et autres poèmes includes an unpublished draft of the poem beginning "Tomb of the wind," which was found among the papers of Georges Henein, to whom Bataille sent it. The draft appears as a separate poem entitled "In the Halo of Death," p. 144. The phrase "halo of death" also appears in Bataille's essay "Sacrifices" (1933), see Inner Experience, p. 75. Variants are indicated below:

112 Tomb of the wind. "In the Halo of Death" begins with these lines:

> In the halo of death
> the streets have horses
> with manes of naked *cocks*

112 you know little ear. "*In the Halo of Death*": you know little old woman.

113 with the crack behind. *In the manuscript (on a piece of calendar paper containing drafts and notes for* The Little One, The Oresteia, *and "Tomb of the wind"), this poem is entitled "Gentle-Bitterness."*

Eliminated Poems and Other Unpublished Poems

Unpublished. Bataille gathered the poems in this section after the publication of "La Discorde" (Discord) in Quatre Vents in September 1945. Written between 1942 and 1945, they are related to the poems published in The Oresteia *and* The Little One, *and to the poems prepared for publication in* The Tomb of Louis XXX. *Our text for these poems is Bataille,* Oeuvres complètes, *vol. 4, pp. 20–26. I have also included a few other unpublished poems from the manuscripts for* Guilty *and* On Nietzsche *in the section as noted below.*

117   at the window of nudity. *Bataille used the first stanza of this poem separately in the "Discord" section of* The Oresteia. *See Bataille,* The Impossible, *trans. Robert Hurley (1962; City Lights Books, 1991), p. 125.*

119   a death rattle. *The final stanza of this poem was published as part of "Discord" prior to the inclusion of that poem in* The Oresteia.

122   and you. *A draft of this poem was found on the back of "The Roman Way," a poem from 1942.*

124   silence without lips. *Dated November 1942, the draft is related to language edited out of a poem in* The Oresteia. *See* The Impossible, *p. 132.*

125   The Window. *Possibly from 1942. This poem appears in a notebook (1942–43?) for* Archangelic, *as one of six poems on separate diary pages. The poems are "The Window," drafts of "Absence of Remorse" from* The Little One, *"Starry depths" from* Disparate Poems, *and "Tomb of the wind" from* The Tomb of Louis XXX. *The final poem in the notebook is this:*

> If you want to be similar
> to death
> you must laugh
> cry
> make love

125   a flat raven. *The notebook draft for this line reads:* a fat raven.

127   and the red knife of the teeth. *This poem was written on the back of the manuscript for "Tears of Frost," see "Me" elsewhere in this volume and* The Impossible, *p. 132.*

128   thirty black asses. *This poem plays with the similarity between "âmes" (souls) and "ânes" (donkeys, asses).*

130   a wooden whore turning a trick. *Possibly from 1942. In the manu-
scripts for* The Oresteia, *on a page from a diary, one finds a crossed
out draft of this poem; the second stanza reads:*

> Dance of whores
> turning round

On the back of the draft, also crossed out:

> Nothingness in a dress
> accompanies the dying
> the dying one sings
> nothingness sings
> and the tomb opens laughing

131   Cracked skull. *Written on the back of the first section of "Heart
greedy to shine." See* The Impossible, *p. 131.*

134   The wolf sighs tenderly. *This poem was found among the manu-
scripts of the* Eliminated Poems, *but the paper and handwriting are
different enough to suggest an alternate date of composition. Our text
for this poem is Bataille,* Oeuvres complètes, *vol. 4, p. 27.*

*The wolf in this poem may recall the wolf in Rimbaud's poem "Le
Loup Criait" (The Wolf Cried), included in* A Season in Hell *as the last
three stanzas of the poem "Faim" (Hunger). A relevant stanza reads: "The
wolf cried under the leaves / while spitting the beautiful feathers / of his
meal of birds: / Like him I consume myself."*

134   a great oak. *The meetings of Acéphale took place around an oak
tree in the Marly forest.*

135   Lost in the thunderheads. *This poem appears in a section of the
manuscript for* Guilty *dated to May 1943. The poem was edited out
of the published version of the book. Our text for this poem is Bataille,*
Oeuvres complètes, *vol. 5, p. 559. See Bataille,* Guilty, *p. 231.*

136   Value in relation to what? *This poem appears in a section of the
manuscript for* On Nietzsche *dated to March 1944. It was edited out*

of the published version of the book. Our text for this poem is Bataille, Oeuvres complètes, *vol. 6, p. 399. See Bataille,* On Nietzsche, *p. 263.*

137   In the space of your heart. *This poem appears in a section of the manuscript for* On Nietzsche *dated to March 1944. It was edited of out the published version of the book. Our text for this poem is Bataille,* Oeuvres complètes, *vol. 6, p. 400. See Bataille,* On Nietzsche, *pp. 263–64.*

137   will I laugh in this sky. *In the notebooks upon which the manuscript of* On Nietzsche *was based:*

Lacerating this immensity
could I still laugh?

137   you are the day. *In the notebook draft:*

you are the cold wind
you are beautiful you are the day

137   it lacerates the naked. *In the notebook draft:* it pierces the naked.

137   the thread the sunlight. *In the notebook draft:* slicing the sunlight.

137   you are the flame that dies. *In the notebook draft:* you are the flame that is born.

137   of naked breasts. *In the notebook draft:* of your crack.

138   Whiteness veiled by damp vapors. *Crossed out:* Barred sky covered with. *This poem appears in a section of the manuscript for* On Nietzsche *dated to June 1944. It was edited out of the published version of the book. Our text for this poem is Bataille,* Oeuvres complètes, *vol. 6, p. 414. See also Bataille,* On Nietzsche, *pp. 277–78.*

138   leaving the untouchable horror naked. *Crossed out:* or naked leaving the inaccessible immensity naked.

138　dead and without beginning or end. *Crossed out:* dead and without foundation or base.

138　burst of my white eyes. *Crossed out:* intolerable sky *[crossed out: causes]* reflection of . . .

138　you are a joke. *In English in the manuscript.*

138　my tears venom *[of?]* my shame. *Crossed out:* sobs, venom, the pus of crime *[shame]*.

139　my feverish hands. *Crossed out:* my hands trembling heavy with ignominy.

139　content with a good turn. *Crossed out:* with demise and dust.

Undifferentiated Being Is Nothing

Published in Botteghe Oscure *13 (1954), pp. 14–16. Bataille's participation in* Botteghe Oscure *came about through his friendship with René Char, who was affiliated with the international journal. Bataille also published essays in* Botteghe Oscure—*including "The Sovereign," "Nonknowledge," and "Pure Happiness"—all of which were associated with* La Somme Athéologique *(see Bataille,* The Unfinished System of Nonknowledge*). There is no manuscript for "Undifferentiated Being Is Nothing," but drafts for the poems appear in a larger group of manuscripts gathered under the title* Erotic Poems. *Our text is Bataille,* Oeuvres complètes, *vol. 3, pp. 367–76.*

143　of felt. *The manuscript of this poem is entitled "Blanchot," and the first two lines read:*

　　Blanchot
　　the felt

143　will disrobe the bones of the dead. *Manuscript:* will disrobe the submerged.

144 of this delirium. *In the manuscript, this poem appears after the one that follows it here.*

146 defunct. *Manuscript:* of a dead man.

147 I puked. *Manuscript title:* The Dead Man. *A first draft, crossed out:*

I puked
through the nose
spider sky
I swallow
the wave that drowns me
the midday sun

These lines recall Zarathustra's "Drunken Song," particularly part 4, sec. 4, of Thus Spoke Zarathustra. *See Nietzsche,* The Portable Nietzsche, *pp. 432ff.*

147 I am dead. *Manuscript:*

take charge of thinning
I was dead.

147 evaporate distilled water. *Manuscript:* exhausted the distilled water.

147 and I fail in the end. *Manuscript:*

not a word
I failed.

Erotic Poems

Unpublished. Written in 1954, in the same notebook as Undifferentiated Being Is Nothing. *Our text appears in Bataille,* Oeuvres complètes, *vol. 4, pp. 28–32.*

153 Insignificance. *In the manuscript for these poems, this poem follows the first poem of* Undifferentiated Being Is Nothing.

155   The Earth. *Manuscript:*

> The dead seized the quick
> and the bird
> closes the procession.

156   The Wash. *In the manuscript for these poems, this poem appears between "The Laws of Taste" and "The Body," two poems used in* Undifferentiated Being Is Nothing.

157   I open the legs. *In the manuscript, these lines are preceded by this draft, crossed out:*

> The Beauty

> In the blood of my heart
> a penis
> and in the vulva
> spurts
> I open the legs
> to the tongue of beef
> of fur

160   sperm swims in blood. *This verse, written in pencil, may be a correction of the preceding one, written in ink.*

160   pantheon of sperm. *In the margin beside these lines, two titles: "Pantheon" and "The Tongue."*

160   from a dull spurt to a sticky one. *In the manuscript, these lines are followed by the poem "The Bald," printed separately below.*

160   my dress to tear open your soul. *Included in the manuscript of* My Mother, *under the title "The Beauty." See Bataille,* Oeuvres complètes, *vol. 4, p. 403. Folded into the manuscript, between this poem and the preceding one: a crossed out draft of the poem "Death Knell" entitled "The Sky" (see below); notes for "La Cavatine" (The Song; see Bataille,* Oeuvres complètes, *vol. 4, pp. 337–38); a crossed out draft of "I Puked" (included in* Undifferentiated Being Is Nothing*).*

161   of the forest. *In the manuscript, this poem is folded between "The Alcohol" and "I Puked" (see* Undifferentiated Being Is Nothing*).*

162   Lightning. *In the manuscript, this poem, entitled "The Storm," is followed by a crossed out draft of "Death Knell," see (b) below.*

166   a long libidinous swing. *In the manuscript this poem is preceded by four crossed out drafts:*

(a)

The Sky

The bronze of love sounds
the red clapper of your prick
in the bell of my cunt

(b)

The clapper of your death knell
in the bell *[crossed out: of my vagina / of my urine]* of
    the cunt
the bronze of love sounds
the long voluptuous swing

(c)

The bronze of love dances
the long voluptuous swing
and the bald clapper of the death knell
sounds and sounds and sounds and sounds
in my libidinous bell

(d)

In my libidinous bell
death's bronze sounds
the clapper of the penis dances
the long voluptuous swing

213

167   The Bald. *The title of this poem, "Le Chauve" (The Bald, The Bald One, The Bald Man) is a euphemism for the penis in French.*

167   of which your testicles are the dawn. *This poem and a short text related to it reappear in the manuscript for* My Mother, *see Bataille,* Oeuvres complètes, *vol. 4, pp. 402–04.*

Coryphea

Unpublished. Found among manuscripts from the 1950s associated with Bataille's projected continuation of La Somme Athéologique *entitled* Le Pur bonheur *(Pure Happiness). See Bataille,* The Unfinished System of Nonknowledge, *p. 237. Our text is Bataille,* Oeuvres complètes, *vol. 4, p. 33.*

Five Poems from 1957

Unpublished. These poems appear in a notebook following a text dated October–November 1957. Our text is Bataille, Oeuvres complètes, *vol. 4, pp. 34–36.*

175   I howl. *In the manuscript, this line begins a new page. The final line of the poem is also followed by a crossed out title, "I Bellow," suggesting that this text may actually be two poems, the second poem beginning with "I Howl."*

177   *Libera nos. From "libera nos domine" (free us Lord).*

179   [The Sidewalk of Danaides]. *The title of this poem was crossed out in the manuscript. The Danaides were the fifty daughters of King Danaas. Their father betrothed them to his fifty nephews but instructed them to murder their husbands on their wedding nights. Purified of those murders at Zeus's request by Hermes and Athena, many of them were later given away as prizes won through competition. They founded the Danaan race. Bataille also references the Danaides in* Guilty, *see Bataille,* Guilty, *pp. 92, 230.*

Index of Titles and First Lines

First lines of poems are italic,
and titles of poems and collections of poetry are roman.

Made in the USA
Las Vegas, NV
22 March 2023

69507457R00148